Confessions of a

Fasting Housewife

One Woman's Journey with Jesus

Catherine Brown

DESTINY IMAGE EUROPE
Via Maiella, 1
66020 San Giovanni Teatino (Ch) - Italy

ISBN: 88-89127-10-4

For Worldwide Distribution
printed in the U.S.A

2 3 4 5 6 7 8/10 09 08 07 06 05

This book and all other Destiny Image Europe books are available at Christian bookstores and distributors worldwide.

To order products, or for any other correspondence:

DESTINY IMAGE EUROPE
Via Acquacorrente, 6
65123 - Pescara - Italy
Tel. +39 085 4716623 - Fax: +39 085 4716622
E-mail: info@eurodestinyimage.com

Or reach us on the Internet:

www.eurodestinyimage.com

Dedication

To women everywhere who love Jesus, chocolate and shoes!

Enjoy.

Contents

Acknowledgement

Vicky—thank you, for believing in me and in this book, and for writing its foreword. Our friendship is a tremendous blessing to me.

Karen—I enjoyed having a fasting buddy. I hope and pray this book will bless you.

Elizabeth and Jess—my heartfelt thanks for your editing skills, proof-reading and insightful comments that led to many positive changes and improvements in the manuscript.

Chantal and Richard—you have both given sacrificially of your time and talents to help me in this project, and I just want to say how much I appreciate each of you.

Francine and our friends and faithful prayer partners of Gatekeepers ministry—I applaud you and thank you for praying me across the finish line of faith. Without your prayers and personal encouragement, this journey would have been much more difficult.

My lovely husband Stephen—a huge "thank you" for your continued support and wisdom and for letting me bounce many ideas off of you. I am so grateful for the depth of love and friendship we share as husband and wife. Thank you, for letting me pursue my God-given desire to write and encourage others. Thanks for all your hard work behind the scenes posting books, fulfilling orders and for all the accounting you do for me. You're a star!

Our children, Mark, Daniel, Rebecca and Samuel—thanks for your smiles, hugs and little notes that say "I love you" that arrive at just the right time!

Little sister—you're not left out of my acknowledgements because you care enough to ask how everything is going. Bless you!

My Lord, Jesus—this book is all about You and how much You mean to me. I thank You, Lord, for Your constant love and faithfulness. You are everything to me.

Foreword

As I read Catherine's book, *Confessions of a Fasting Housewife*, I felt as though I were feasting at a banquet table. Even though this is a book about fasting, I felt as if I were dining at a table filled with great delicacies from my heavenly Father of mercy, grace and love.

This book is truly a gift to the Body of Christ. God has lavished us with the gift of Catherine's vulnerability, and He has comforted us with the grace that flows from her day-to-day struggles and longings. She has opened her heart and laid bare her feelings, so we would be lifted up and drawn closer to Jesus.

Catherine truly has an anointing to assist others in loving God. Through her honesty and humility, she untangles and tears down the religious complications of loving Him. Catherine makes loving Him a simple and pleasurable experience once again. As we share details of her life, we cannot help but be pulled into a realm of longing for Him. *Confessions of a Fasting Housewife* is a masterpiece of mercy that will open your heart and mind to receive the grace to love God more than ever before.

This is not just another book about fasting—indeed, it is a journey of grace! I found myself captivated by Catherine's life. I applauded her victories, laughed with delight at her housewife jargon and wept over the revelations she shares. The more I read, the more I had to read; I was unable to put it down. I felt like I had crawled into the lap of God, and became wrapped in His arms of love. I wholeheartedly endorse *Confessions of a Fasting Housewife*, and I know that this wonderful book will forever bless and change your life as it has mine. Catherine Brown is a very dear sister whose prophetic voice is a fresh breeze—her love for God is contagious!

Love and blessings,

Victoria Boyson
Speaking Life Ministries
Cedar Rapids, Iowa
www.boyson.org

Introduction

*T*his book is a testimony to God's ability to bring a child of His own through the doorway of divine opportunity and launch her into the race of faith. It is a tale of tenderness and—being true to life—is full of laughter and tears.

A TIME OF DISCOVERY AND DELIGHT

When I was young, my little sister and I liked to dress up in my mother's high-heeled shoes and parade around the house, while wearing her best beads and pretty lipstick. There is nothing quite as satisfying to a small girl as the "clack-clack-clack" sound of high heels on floorboards! This was not an everyday occurrence, but something that we enjoyed from time to time. We had such fun dipping into special boxes, and digging out the much sought after jewelry and cosmetics.

This was a time of discovery and delight for two small daughters, with only the odd, minor mishap. For instance, we would occasionally lose our balance and topple over on the stilettos, because we were not used to traipsing around in high-heeled shoes. We may have sustained the odd, bumped kneecap, but that never stopped us from trying to emulate our precious mom. We dreamed of growing up and being beautiful. We pretended to be princesses and enjoyed every moment. The desire to be elegant beckoned us to womanhood and maturity.

LEARNING SOMETHING FOR THE FIRST TIME, TAKES TIME

When we were young we sprayed on expensive scents from glass bottles with puffer applicators, and applied eye shadow, blush and lipstick to our faces as though make-up was going out of fashion. As little girls often do when learning, we missed the defining outlines of our eyes, cheeks and lips while liberally smearing cosmetics all over our faces. Slowly, we began to realize that the whole process wasn't as easy as mom had made it look. In the process of our mini-makeovers, we began to understand that learning a new skill initially takes time and effort, and that the pathway to successful transformation is paved with a measure of skill and patience.

My mom had a small gold locket that used to catch my eye. On the outside was an etched, single stem rose with a small red garnet stone within. Inside the oval locket, mom had inserted some precious photographs. Something about this particular piece of jewelry grabbed my attention. Perhaps, the secret surprise of finding family pictures inside, or that it looked so pretty around my mother's neck is what tugged at my heart. I liked to borrow and wear this locket so I could look just as she did. I wanted to reflect the beauty I saw—both in her and the rose.

The process described in *Confessions of a Fasting Housewife* is similar to the progression of change that I have described above, but with an emphasis on a person's inner beauty and God's method of transformation. Just as I wanted to emulate my mom when I was a little girl, I believe that every Christian desires to reflect the beauty seen in our Lord Jesus Christ. This book is a heavenly jewelry box full of tiny love trinkets and tokens of divine affection.

As children, my sister and I were overjoyed to dress up and play with jewelry and cosmetics. These were experiences that represented our taking some first, tentative steps into the relatively unknown realms of womanhood. It is now my joy—as a fully-grown woman—to warmly invite you to join me on a journey of personal discovery about yourself and Jesus. In gentleness, the Lord will adorn you with His beautiful virtues and cover you with the fragrance of Heaven. As you gaze into His eyes, you will reflect His love just as a mirror perfectly reveals the image before it.

CHAPTER 1

'Dear Diary'

*T*his book is about miniature miracles, which matter as much to God as do the bigger ones. I hope both men and women will enjoy *Confessions of A Fasting Housewife*, but I am not ashamed to say that its written from a woman's perspective, with her identity in Christ in mind. Therefore, it may appeal more to female readers than male ones. As well as sharing spiritual truths, I have described some of my life's more humdrum aspects. My desire is to be realistic about many facets of my lifestyle, so as to encourage people—especially women—to press into their Kingdom destiny.

Spirituality is not impractical. The Lord can, and does, work through our busy schedules, as we shop, cook, clean house, do the laundry, kiss bruises, answer the telephone, go to work, clean toilets, attend meetings and so on. I appreciate that, for some readers, the sharing of such details may be slightly boring. But, I want to state that God reigns supreme through the mundane and the mediocre!

Confessions of A Fasting Housewife is a candid collection of diary entries during my first attempt at a 40-day food fast. I say "attempt," because I didn't actually make it to day 40, but there is more on that later. The fact that I even made it as far as day 33 is a minor miracle in itself. For now, I am content to extend an invitation for you to read my correspondence with Heaven. It contains pages written on my heart as I did diaries of my ups-and-downs of life, as recorded during my fasting experience. Perhaps, while reading, you will, like me, make discoveries about yourself that you never knew. Should you wish to write a journal, I hope that the Lord uses the process to bless you, and that your completed diary entries will be a joyful reminder of what God is doing in your life.

INVITATION NOT INVASION

My daughter Rebecca keeps a diary adorned with the tantalizing title, "Private. Keep out. It's boring anyway." Once or twice, when I've been tidying her room and come across it, I've been tempted to take a peek—who hasn't when confronted with the unknown? It's quite tempting to follow our natural curiosity through to its obvious conclusion. When we discover a diary, our curiosity is aroused. What secrets will be contained within its pages? Will we discover something new about the person and/or ourselves? Will it be a good surprise, or will it bring a shocking revelation?

We are intrigued by what makes each other tick, especially those whom we love. So far, I've managed to leave Rebecca's secrets neatly locked away because—despite the temptation to look—I don't want to invade her privacy. I would much rather wait and receive her invitation. Her permission means everything to me. With permission, we become legitimate partakers with each other while on life's journey, as opposed to being uninvited intruders.

But, perhaps, the thought of writing down your private thoughts and meditations initially fills you with uncertainty and apprehension? I also used to feel the same way. When I was a little girl, I never kept a diary. I was afraid that if I wrote down my innermost secrets, someone would find them, read them and, ultimately, disapprove. We all want to be liked and loved by those around us. Have you ever accidentally (or purposely) listened to a conversation that others are having about you, and then heard something unflattering about yourself? Or, perhaps, you have been tempted to make an unflattering comment about another person: once caught with a red face and guilty lips, you've blurted out an apology. Most of us, at one time or another, have made or received disclosures that were unkind. This fact tends to cloud our self-perspective and can prevent us from sharing openly in the future.

For instance, I once found, quite by accident, an e-mail written by my husband to a male friend. In the message, he openly shared his heart about being relieved that his grumpy wife (me?!) had gone shopping! I was extremely hurt when I read this. I had caught him in the act of sharing something completely un-edifying (although true on this occasion) with another. The e-mail was about two years old when I came across it. This discovery may have been initially unpleasant, but it helped me to grasp how horrible I had been and how my behavior effected Stephen more than I realized. My husband has since apologized for breaking my trust, and I have set a personal goal of being less grumpy! Reading the truth is good—even if it stings a bit—because, just like salt in a wound, it ultimately brings purification and healing. This fasting experience has accomplished something similar in my heart.

CONSEQUENCES AND COMPLIMENTS

As a child in the sixth grade of elementary school, I learned the consequences of writing inappropriately. The children in class were playing a rather mischievous game that, funnily enough, was called "Consequences." It involved writing down the name of our teacher, as well as that of another teacher, and then selecting a place for them to meet. One child would write a detail, then fold the paper over and pass it to the next child, and so on. The offending article was once discovered in my possession, just before I could pass it to the next student. When the teacher read the letter, his face turned scarlet with rage. Corporal punishment had not yet been banned from our schools, and, as a penalty for my "misdemeanor," my hands received two lashings from a leather belt.

Once during a high school English class, a secret admirer had written a note about me, and was passing it across his desk to another boy. I was quite unaware of either the admirer or his love note—until the teacher noticed what was going on and confiscated his message. I was thoroughly embarrassed by its contents, even though the boy was trying to give me compliments.

As a lovesick teenager, I broke my own "no diary" rule and began penning "puppy love" thoughts on scraps of school notebook paper. Can you imagine my dismay when my mom unwittingly discovered them, and then scolded me for being too intense? Even though I was a silly 15-year-old in love for the first time, what I had written was precious nonetheless. It was part of who I was, and writing it down saved me from an emotional implosion. These unexpected disclosures caused the awkward, clumsy child inside me to consider never venturing down the path of written confession ever again. For a time, "Dear Diary" was confined to reading other people's thoughts in the "true-to-life" glossy picture stories in teenage magazines.

THE LITERARY BUTTERFLY EMERGES

Gradually, however, the emerging writer inside me gained some footage. I overcame my fear as my pen flowed like a rushing river. I started corresponding with pen friends, and thoroughly enjoyed getting to know a lovely German girl. I also received romantic letters from a young Dutch man, and even had two marriage proposals from two other male pen friends—from a Chilean man and an American G.I. Eventually, I came to understand that not all written disclosures carried a penalty! Writing and receiving letters was great fun, and the magic salve of self-expression through written words worked wonders for my confidence. The letters and cards that I gave and received expressed friendship, love, hope and humor. My friends and I shared lessons learned in life, and we empathized and encouraged each other along the way. Therefore, I hope that sharing my journal will uplift and encourage you too.

BRIDAL INTIMACY

One of the most romantic letters I ever received was a handwritten note from my husband during our engagement—it contained the following poetic line, *"I love you more times than the sea hits the shore"* and had the infinity symbol written next to my future bridegroom's signature. Likewise, the story within this book is one of unending bridal love and intimacy. It reflects various aspects of my life with Christ, including my roles and duties as a daughter, a wife, a mother, a friend and a minister of the gospel. This transparent dialogue is one covered in Jesus' love and that reflects His heart for the Church, which is His bride.

THE MIRACLE OF LOVE AND ACCEPTANCE

Our youngest son, Samuel, has a great way of telling you how he feels. He says, "Mommy, I love you AND I like you too." Now, I can also say this: I love myself and I like myself. Ultimately, I have found a place of security in God, and know that I can be myself and that I am lovely because He created me in His image. My prayer is also for you to have this reality resonate throughout your entire being.

I encourage you to freely enter this journey with me without fear of reprisal. I willingly and lovingly share my diary and, therefore, my life with you. If you need permission, then it is unconditionally granted. The fledgling duckling I once was has been altered into a graceful swan, who is now wrapped in a garland of God's grace. I believe that God wants to create a safe and loving environment where you too can consider what is both common and Kingdom-minded, and through that process may enjoy inner transformation.

CHAPTER 2

What Is Fasting?

I am grateful that our household is able to have three regular meals a day, and that I can snack in between meals as much as I like. Much to the horror of my increasing waistline, chocolate cake and potato chips are two of my favorite snacks. With this in mind, I suppose I should be considered one of the most unqualified people in the universe to write a book on fasting! Allow me to explain, however. If any successful steps are to be taken before, during and even after a fast, I stumbled upon them more by accident than design. God, however, graciously carried me towards the faith goal.

So, what exactly is fasting? *The Oxford Dictionary* defines it as "abstinence from food or water especially as a religious observance." At times, my imagination has come up with outrageous excuses on why NOT to fast. It's been refreshing to honestly face my flesh, and let God sort out some of my occasionally crackpot reasons. Sometimes, I simply couldn't be bothered to fast, or I would use being busy as an excuse. Other times, I fasted with great faith goals in mind. But then, I gave up—a few hours or a few days into my fast—after being lured away by the irresistible aroma of toast. However, with perseverance and huge portions of God's grace, I gradually built up to missing more than one meal at a time. From there, I pushed for longer fasting periods. In the process, I realized that I wouldn't die if I missed one meal—although you might have thought so by listening to my self-pitying moans!

After my first successful attempt at sharing a fast with others, I felt confident enough to try it alone for slightly longer periods. My one to three day fasts gradually extended into five-day fasts. From there, I somehow managed to stagger to the finish line of a whole week without food. The first time I completed a seven-day fast, I felt utterly exhausted, as though I had climbed a mountain. During this particular one, I was fasting for a financial breakthrough in a personal project. At one point, I almost gave up. At that desperate time, I lied on my bed and asked God for help. He responded, and His grace flooded my being, including my rumbling stomach. By the end of that week, I remember thinking that I would never be the same again. How true I had been!

Sometimes, fasting has caused me extreme embarrassment. On one occasion, my hunger made me tearful, gave me a headache and stomach cramps. I had also experienced bouts of diarrhea. Nonetheless, I was determined to continue. While serving my family their evening meal, I had "an accident" at the dinner table! I screamed with shock, told them what had happened and then we all collapsed in laughter. There was nothing else to do—either I could laugh or break down and cry in absolute humiliation. I decided not to take the situation, or myself, too seriously and the laughter enabled me to push through physical discomfort to the end of my fast. Joy and laughter, which are definitely part of God's gift to us, are particularly important while fasting.

Having shared some of fasting's less attractive aspects, you might wonder why any sane person would want to fast. That's a reasonable question; this book may leave you with several unanswered questions, and I do not presume to know the right answers, or even the right questions to ask in the first place. However, I gladly share with you the heart knowledge I have accumulated on the subject of fasting. I do this in the hopes of encouraging you to run the race of faith.

I believe that fasting is personal, and its effects are as individual as you are. There are times when God calls a group of people to fast corporately around a common cause. But that command still requires each individual within that body of believers to make a personal choice to fast. The how, when, where and why of fasting are yours to inquire directly of the Lord.

Lots of people fast for various reasons, but what does fasting actually accomplish? In a nutshell, my experience of fasting is that it causes change.

Fasting causes 'something" to happen that is usually God-inspired, and makes a huge positive difference to a person or a situation. Despite the physical inconveniences one may experience while fasting, it does release a tremendous blessing, bounty and breakthrough from God. Ultimately, fasting draws us nearer to Christ—it is a key that unlocks heavenly treasure chests that are filled with untold blessing.

How fasting actually works involves a certain mystery, but it's all part of the compelling aspect of this Kingdom pearl of great value. We can never truly understand all God's thoughts, for His ways are so much higher than ours. Yet incredibly, He still invites us to partner with Him. Choosing to fast is an act of humility. As we make this choice, God gently meets us and lifts us into fresh dimensions of revelation and relationship with Him. Fasting is a bridge—a divine connector—which carries us deep into the recesses of the Father heart of God. During a fast, the Father gently turns our faces towards His own. Fasting is a tool, and also a treasure box. Sometimes, fasting is the only way forward when the status quo of a circumstance needs to be broken.

We may liken fasting to a mother giving birth. The process of childbirth entails a natural progression from discomfort and pain into the indescribable joy of giving birth and then holding the long-awaited baby for the first time. No words could ever adequately express the intimacy of this moment. So it is with fasting. Momentary physical discomforts soon give way to spiritual joys. The method of transition can be painful at times, but it is always worthwhile. What a gift a child is. Likewise, what a gift we find in fasting for our beloved King.

CHAPTER 3

The Kleenex Fast

*I*am desperate to see Jesus glorified through more salvations and miracles being released on the earth. When I think of Jesus, I see the beautiful Man Christ and all the miracles intertwined in His compassion and mercy, and that flow from His heart of love. Before beginning my fast, I anticipated that if I fasted for 40 days (as did the Lord) then I would come out of my personal wilderness, be clothed in power and be ready to do mighty miracles in His name. The result looked far different from how I had imagined. Surprisingly enough, I cried a lot. In fact, if I chose to describe this particular experience, I would name it the "Kleenex"* fast!

Let me explain how the Lord uses tears in my life. Sometimes, I weep tears of compassion when the Lord moves my heart with His mercy. At other times, the cause of my weeping is not spiritual, but due to being physically exhausted or under extreme stress. Crying is simply my way of letting off steam and stopping me from internalizing everything—it's a release valve, if you like. So I openly state that I am a person who is occasionally given to tears. I have learned that I don't have to be afraid of my emotions; I must simply surrender them to Christ and invite him to be Lord over them. We are to be led by the Spirit, and not by our emotions.

Throughout this fast, I was tired—extremely weak in a physical sense—and sometimes struggled to meet the demands on my time. Jesus permitted my emotions to undergo a beating, which was covered in His grace. Despite red eyes and a bloated nose, I emerged at the other end with a sense of victory and a greater reliance on God than I had ever known, and not to mention a more slender exterior!

During my fast, I had hoped to completely abstain from food. But fairly early on, I became so physically exhausted that I had to compromise and, instead, settle for a greatly reduced food intake. I gave up about three-quarters of the way through finishing (on Day 33), which was a week short of my initial 40-day goal. For a day or two, I saw this as failure, but quickly came to realize that this wasn't God's point of view. Jesus is gracious to receive our best efforts, even if we consider them failures. It's sensible to know when to surrender. Fasting isn't meant to be a punishment or a penance, but rather a gift from God.

Despite these lovely words of promise, during this particular fast I was grumpier than I ever thought a person could be when doing something "for" Jesus. Some fast you might say! Yet, it is surprising how typical my experiences are of those who surrender to the fasting process. Having the ugly side of our fallen human nature come rising to the surface seems to be part-and-parcel of the process. Fasting acts a bit like a sieve on your self; if you will permit, the Holy Spirit will gently shake both sin and self out of you to make more room for His glory to dwell.

It is both a terrible and wonderful experience to be confronted with the darkness of one's heart in His holy presence, but then experience blessings of the Lord's righteousness. I've come to realize that despite the grimace and grudge of my weak flesh, the Holy Spirit can, and ultimately does, reveal God's glory, if I let Him. Amidst all my whimpering reigns a glorious God!

Despite, or sometimes because of, my weaknesses, I had profound encounters with God, and entered into new levels of surrender and

God-dependence. His graciousness almost overwhelmed me at times, as I learned to receive more of His tender mercies. My faith levels rose, and I'm now hungrier for miracles (excuse the pun) than ever before. What began as a decision in faith-filled discipline was, ultimately, revealed to my heart as a precious gift from God.

Having firmly established that I am certainly no expert at fasting, it's probably also accurate to say that I am willing to "have a go," as it were. In doing so, I hope that God has been able to use even the most unlikely candidate to accomplish His will. With this in mind, I feel sufficiently released from any sense of inadequacy to narrate the chronicles of a fasting housewife. Hopefully, amidst the tears, tantrums and laughter, these narratives will prove to be of great value. Be blessed!

I prepared for this 40-day fast in my usual style; in other words, I didn't really make any sensible preparations. The most appropriate way of preparing for a fast—extended or otherwise—is to gradually reduce food and caffeine intake; thus, you gently prepare the body by cutting down food consumption in measured fashion before beginning. However, I have a tendency to eat right up to the last minute, and then suffer for this in the first few days of fasting. This fast was no exception to my usual lunatic, lack of proper preparation. My birthday falls on October 23rd, which just happened to be a few days before I began my chosen fast. On the evening of October 27th, I devoured lots of delicious chocolates and a glass of red wine, all of which had been given as birthday presents.

Although I was physically unprepared for this fast, I did feel spiritually ready. I had spent the past two years debating with the Holy Spirit about the impossibility of doing a long fast, since I thought I could never complete it. In the end, I had to make a decision to "have a go," and trust that His grace (2 Corinthians 12:9) was sufficient for even the most reluctant of potential fasters, and this included me!

Endnotes

* Kleenex – a brand name for paper tissues

CHAPTER 4

The First Week

DAY 1 – Monday, October 28th 2002

God's grace is amazing. Despite my ridiculous lack of physical preparation for this fast, I have no stomach cramps and no headache. Good is good. I believe that I am to begin a fresh study on the Cross. I am anticipating great revelation from my Master. Teach me, Rabbi, Your servant is listening.

Fasting for Breakthrough

I am fasting for miracles. That is my heart. I am desperate for a miracle anointing for the sick, the wounded, the weary, the lost and the broken-hearted. Today, I desire to see the full release of the power of Jesus and His Kingdom come, so that many lives will be restored and countless souls won for Christ. I seek His face with all my heart, and I know that there is so much more to experience of Jesus' love. Such is the mystery of the Kingdom. I want my life to reflect Jesus, no more and no less. Oh, Father, hear my prayer.

DAY 2 – Tuesday, October 29th

Still no cramps or headache, but I am voraciously thirsty. I am drinking lots of water, but I don't seem to be able to quench my thirst. I think of Jesus and His life-giving waters welling up within me to become a fountain of life. Dear Holy Spirit, please fill and refresh me.

Two years ago, I attempted an "Esther Fast." Queen Esther fasted for three days, during which time she did not consume any food or water (see Esther 4:16). Nothing whatsoever! At this time, I was involved in another national prayer event and truly wanted to join my young prayer warriors in fasting. I only managed to sustain 20 hours of total abstinence before giving in and having a drink of water, followed by a piece of toast. I was disappointed that I had completed less than one-third of my allotted 72 hour fast of total abstinence. But I resolved that Jesus was blessed by the fact that I had at least tried. Jesus loves our acts of selfless faith, even if they don't look quite how we had initially anticipated.

I am asking the Lord what He wants to teach me during this time. He has spoken the word "endurance" to me. How does that differ from perseverance? He has taught me perseverance through many situations before, and I have learned to be like the widow in Luke 18. I sense that endurance has more of an edge to the suffering aspect. Yikes! The Bible says if we share in Christ's suffering, then we will also reign with Him (see 2 Timothy 2:12). Lord, I believe your Word. I believe that if I share—even in some tiny way—in fellowship with Your suffering, then I will move in Your kingly anointing, and that means miracles and salvations—all for Your glory my precious Lord. (*Note to self*: Compared to Jesus, I know nothing at all about suffering.)

I read about the Cross today, and I thought "How astounding that the people would reject You as their King." I can hardly comprehend it. Why could they not see Your beauty and majesty? Yet, Lord, there was a time when I, like them, rejected Your lordship and sovereign rule in my life. Your Kingdom comes in me as I surrender to Your kingly authority and dominion.

The Word says they considered You worthy of death. The Cross is the place of death, sacrifice and outrageous grace and love. In my Bible, I turn to the Book of Revelation and lose myself in worship of the Sacrificial Lamb. You are worthy to open the scroll, only You are worthy Lord. No other could take Your place. My heart explodes with love for You. (In the natural, I find that in my conversation, I am starting to speak utter gibberish. I try to string cohesive sentences together, and end up saying things back-to-front and front-to-back! It's difficult to concentrate.)

DAY 3 – Wednesday, October 30th

My thirst persists. I am astounded that I have no diarrhea. Normally, I have a horrible stomach pains by the third day, but, blissfully, I haven't had any this fast. My head hurts a lot today, but I am grateful that is my only side effect. Still, it is uncomfortable and I feel pretty yucky.

I am hungry, but I am sick of tea and coffee. They are probably not the most sensible things to drink while fasting, but with my schedule I like the caffeine kick! Running the house and the ministry are energy consuming. The devil is hot on my heels and is thundering out shouts of health risks. I do wonder if I should have sought medical advice before beginning such a long fast. I am beginning to waiver. Am I doing the right thing? I think of going to the doctor's and trying to explain what I am doing. I cringe at the thought of a lecture. I decide to go to the doctor's office, but then I change my mind again. God's love is enough! He will sustain me!

A close friend announces she has also started a 40-day fast. Much to my surprise, my first response is that I feel slightly annoyed! How weird is that? The Lord reveals more pride in my heart. Did I believe that I was the only one who loved Him enough, or had the desire in my heart to please Him? How outrageous—I am convicted. In retrospect, I am delighted that I have a friend to share this time with. I pray that it will not become competitive between us, and that we can bless and encourage each other as we go along. Please help me to be humble, Lord.

Alone again, I meditate on the events that lead to Your crucifixion. You were betrayed and called a sinner friend. Oh, Judas, how tragic that you were the one. How catastrophic that you betrayed your greatest friend. Friendship and betrayal are on my mind. The Bible says that the Sanhedrin were envious of You. Oh, Lord, even Pilate could see it, but not the religious people of the day. You are showing me that envy is at the heart of betrayal. Lord, help me to forgive those who may betray me and to respond as You did. Lord, deliver me from the temptation to be envious. You said to Judas, "Friend, do what you came for" (Matthew 26:50). Even in betrayal, You were ever the Prince of Peace. How I love You.

At dinner tonight, I drank some vegetable juice from the bowl of peas. It smelled so good as I sat down with the family at mealtime. We roared with laughter at my ridiculous antics. Rebecca and Samuel drank some too and we decided that it was delicious.

Tonight, I ministered to a young man who was seeking the baptism of the Holy Spirit. Unless we are born again, we cannot enter the Kingdom. We worshiped and prayed together, and the Lord met him powerfully. I felt his spirit awaken. Thank You, Father!

DAY 4 – Thursday, October 31ˢᵗ

My breath is awful and it stinks! I had to buy Airwaves chewing gum because my mouth smells so bad.

Witches, Warlocks and a Lily from God

On Halloween, J. K. Rowling (author of the wildly successful *Harry Potter* books) is hosting a charity ball at Stirling Castle to support multiple sclerosis (MS). The castle is to be decorated in the style of Hogwart's School of Wizardry and witches will be in attendance; I don't know if they are actors or actual practicing witches. The guest list is exclusive and private and each person is being asked to fork out £250 per ticket.

Last Saturday, after a powerful time of intercession against the spirit of witchcraft, the Lord melted my heart (on Sunday) with His compassion for J. K. Rowling. I read an article about how she is the patron of multiple sclerosis in Scotland. The reason is that, in 1990, her mother died from MS at the age of 45. Furthermore, the article stated that this is why Harry Potter is an orphan and the subject of death is featured so much in her books: she never got over the death of her mother. I see a broken-hearted little girl who is so in need of the Father's tender-loving care. We are all spiritual orphans, until we are reconciled to our heavenly Father.

Love is Spiritual Warfare!

For more than a year, I have been praying and asking the Lord for His heart for J.K. Rowling, but I have never truly felt the depth of His compassion for her, until now. I had thought of going to Stirling Castle on the day of Halloween to pray against the spirit of witchcraft, but the Lord said to me: *"Child, this is your act of spiritual warfare—to send a bouquet of flowers in My name and express my love to JKR."* I was stunned—I thought that was wimpy! How much I have to learn. Eventually, after praying with Stephen, and then some more on my own, I saw the Lord's hand in the flowers. It is to be my deepest joy to send a bouquet of flowers to J. K. Rowling via Stirling Castle. Thank You, Father.

The intercessory warfare against witchcraft has been powerful. My combat this time will be equally powerful. I have sent a simple bouquet of white lilies with a single red rose in their midst. The card that accompanies them states, "God cares for you (John 3:16), from a friend who knows His outrageous grace, Catherine Brown." I put "friend" because Jesus is a friend to sinners. If this is my Lord's way, then it must also be mine—for perfect forgiveness is ours through Christ.

The way that we show love to others is a measure of how much the reality of what God has forgiven us is being worked out in our lives. I am comforted by Paul's letter to the Corinthians, which is a revelation of love in action: what love is and how love works. Love IS the greatest act of spiritual warfare. (I started reading "The Bride," which is an allegory of the Song of Songs. I found it difficult to get into initially, but now I am blessed. I believe it will help sustain me in the days to come.)

Wanting to Give Up

Today was difficult: I almost gave up my fast, which was strange for me because usually day three is agony, and then everything is okay on day four. But not this time. My greatest need is for fresh bread: the smell of bread is driving me crazy.

Stephen hugged me this morning, and laughed and said, "You are losing weight." I didn't begin this fast to improve what I looked like on the outside, but losing a few pounds would be delightful. It's great to have my husband compliment me on my new, leaner look, but I am hungry for inner transformation. Rebecca asked me if I would lose weight during my fast. I told her, "I'm not sure." We'll see what size I am in 36 days.

I've added lump-free soup to my intake of liquids, as well as the occasional liquid yogurt drink. I gave up on Bovril, because it was making me too thirsty. Having hot soup is such a treat! It's made sitting with the family so much easier at meal times. Our family time is important, and we all usually sit together at meal times to share the day's events around the table. To miss out on that doesn't seem right. I don't want to lose my prayer time with Jesus, but I am trying to carry on as normal as possible. I am sure that the Lord will honor this. I resist the urge to fall into condemnation or be legalistic. My life is a prayer, and the prayers will flow through that lifestyle choice.

Go to Bed Sleepy Head

I am finding that I easily grow tired and that my energy levels are low. Evenings find me needing to go to bed earlier. Stephen is so kind and understanding. I just cannot stay awake the same way that I used to. We cuddle up and laugh as my stomach rumbles noisily. I feel Stephen's support keenly and it helps me to carry on. In the mornings, I am more sluggish than usual and need to make a conscious decision to engage with the Spirit and allow my flesh to be refined in the process.

The Bridegroom & The Cross

I continue to fervently seek revelation of the Cross. Sometimes, Lord, I just blankly stare at the pages of Your Word. I see the words, but not the fresh revelation I am in anguish for. I know that there is more to see. As I slip in and out of sleep, You begin to speak to my spirit and show me many aspects of Your nature and character: through the Passover supper; the intercession at Gethsemane; and then the Resurrection and Ascension.

In this moment, I cannot see You as the Bridegroom at the Cross. Oh, I need to see You as the Bridegroom at the Cross. You are so gracious to me. Then the revelation comes: *"Child, as you gaze upon the Cross, where I waited nailed by Perfect Love, I waited at the altar as your Bridegroom. There in the place of sorrow and suffering, I waited as a faithful Bridegroom for My bride."*

I cry—it is such a perfect picture of divine love, my Bridegroom King. How costly was the dowry that we might be betrothed to You. Help me to remember the price You paid, and to not turn away when You ask me to count the cost of loving You and to embrace the Cross. I choose to surrender and obey. I want to emulate Your sacrificial love in action.

They called You the King of the Jews; You are my King and the king of the universe. Let countless others embrace the reality of Your love my Lord. Call Your Church to intimacy, and through this royal relationship bring her into bridal rule. Clothe the Church in virtue. Turn our hearts to embrace Your love. Cause us to be lovesick—not in a silly, sentimental way—but as a passionate, burning reality as Your Kingdom is fused into our beings.

DAY 5 – Friday, November 1st

I am Weak, But He is Strong

I am so utterly and desperately weak. My knees fail me. I cannot even string together two cohesive sentences. But He is strong, although I am weak. I lean on Jesus because, quite frankly, I don't trust my own strength right now. "Hallelujah," I hear Heaven resound!

We've been for our usual weekly trip to McDonald's—it's a Friday night indulgence for the entire family. It was pouring wet outside, and Mark was in a bit of a mood. I wasn't sure how I would handle this time, because it's always a treat for me to not have to cook, and the kids just love chicken nuggets and French fries. I decided to have a strawberry milkshake, but it was too thick and I felt sick. I didn't feel upset or annoyed, it just felt strange to be in McDonald's and not eat anything. I am losing some desire for food. I have decided to leave out yogurt drinks, because they don't settle too well in my stomach.

DAY 6 – Saturday, November 2nd

I attended a meeting with ministers from the region. The time together was precious—we got to wash each other's feet with prayer. But the evening was difficult. My stomach rumbled so much, and I was hungrier than I had been up to this point. It's actually amazing how little I have felt famished. Tonight, I felt as though I were starving. I tried some Lucozade, but that just made my breath worse and it increased my thirst. Despite all of this, the physical weakness is beginning to lift slightly.

The Dream

I had a dream in the night: I was dressed in an exquisite bridal gown with attendants, and then I was brought before Jesus my King. I wore the golden crown that You once gave me in a vision before, Lord. On two separate occasions, You have given me different stones, which have been fitted into the crown. The first gem You gave to me was a pearl for wisdom; the second stone was a diamond that represented a revival anointing. You give each of us a crown of salvation so that we can throw it down in adoration at Your feet, just as the 24 elders described in the Book of Revelation.

Tonight, Lord, You held a glowing light in Your hands. You told me to bow down, and then You placed the light in my crown. I asked you what it was and you replied, *"It is the light of My glory."* You explained that it had to be kept covered, except for the times You would permit it to be revealed. Two angels then came and placed dark garments around me. These garments—which were shaped somewhat like an old sack—represented humility. A veil was also placed over my face. You showed me times to come Lord. I saw into the future where many thousands of souls were gathered. The veil was removed from my face, and the light of Your glory was revealed. Many people were saved, because they saw Your glory. Oh, Lord, I am without words. You said that for each week I manage to fast, there will be a similar encounter and further impartation. Thank You, Lord, for the gift of humility and glory to Your Church.

I believe this dream is not only for me, but is representative of the Bride of Christ and the end time anointing You are pouring out on her Lord. The revelation You are giving to me is available to any believer who loves You. Your word says that we reveal Your glory with unveiled faces. Let Your light shine in the nations as Your Church reaches out in compassion to the lost souls.

DAY 7 – Sunday, November 3rd

I took the children to my niece's birthday party. There was lots of lovely smells and delicious food around. I allowed myself a treat—a hot chocolate. It was delicious, and carried me through the party atmosphere in a great mood! I think I will drink more milk—it's probably good for me right now. As I looked around me at the many people at the party, I felt as if I were looking through Your eyes, Jesus. I don't seem to be myself any more. It's as though I am gone, and only You are looking out. My heart is bursting with Your compassion, which is a key to unlocking the miraculous.

Nothing to Take to the Cross

Lord, You are speaking more to me about embracing the Cross. I know I need to see it from a fresh perspective. At times, I am so slow. I look and look, and see nothing new and what I do see seems somehow blurred. I am longing for fresh revelation. You've spoken to my heart and said, *"Child I took nothing with me to the Cross—no praise of man, no ministry accolades, no favor with man—only My father's blessing and approval. If you wish to embrace the Cross fully, you too must take nothing to the Cross."*

I am challenged, but willing. Oh, Lord, make me like you. You call the Church to take up her cross, and with single-minded devotion be dedicated to You and Your ways. It is not about self-denial, but about denial of self. Self-denial applied without grace may never penetrate the heart and effects only surface change, whereas denial of self is the place of deepest transformation as grace works out surrender to Your Kingdom, which comes into our yielded hearts.

A desire for bread is driving me nuts. I almost shoved an entire slice of bread into my mouth while making packed lunches for the kids to take to school. God gave me grace to resist the enticement. I have found spiritual temptation so strong today. The longest I have ever been able to fast completely from food is seven days, but I have crossed a threshold today. The devil has tried to trick me into saying that I have done well in coming this far and that the Lord won't mind if I give up now. I know there will be no condemnation in Jesus if I stopped now, but I also realize that I will miss out on some of His blessing if I do.

CHAPTER 5

Week Two: Counting the Cost

DAY 8 – Monday, November 4th

*I*am trying to organize myself to see if I can attend the British and Irish Prayer Leaders gathering. It's not the easiest place to reach. I found a cheap flight, and the organizers are happy to offer me a scholarship to help defray the costs. But I don't seem to be able to get any peace in my heart about attending. Can I really justify spending around £40 and taking a whole day/evening out on the day before our Ladies' Outreach on December 4th? I am not certain that I can.

I am unsure what to do, Lord. I want to continue to network with other prayer leaders/evangelists and build relationships. Am I still kidding myself? Is this still more about me than it is about you, Lord? Oh, Jesus, please help me discern. I'll pray with Stephen—He usually has the final word of wisdom if I am unsure.

The Scars of Christ

In a vision, the Lord asked me to look at the Cross and tell Him what I saw. I saw a wooden cross. He said, *"No child look at me and what do you see."* I looked again, and then I saw His head and scars. I get a fresh revelation about the scars on Your face, Jesus. I cannot believe I haven't thought about it more before now. You wore a crown of thorns for me to wear a crown of glory. I've understood this before, but never looked closely enough at Your head to notice the many scars under Your beautiful hairline where thorns pierced Your flesh. Your scars are an eternal reminder to me of Your suffering. How could I not have seen their splendor as clearly before? Your blood-bought crown is the seal of Your sovereign rule in my life, and a sign of the joy set before You while You endured the Cross (Hebrews 12:2).

Fasting is about Worship and Surrender

I get some further revelation. I can leave this place of suffering anytime. Myrrh is a spice that speaks of death-to-self and sacrificial obedience, and it was part of the embalming ointment used on Jesus' dead body (see John 19:3). I am not forced to stay here. His love does not demand it. However, I know that if I leave now, I will miss out on what He has for me in this time and place.

Christ the Divine Demander

His love only asks, but never demands. As I pursue this thought, I realize that the Kingdom does demand a decision in one respect only. Jesus preached, "Repent, for the kingdom of heaven is near" (Matthew 4:17). You come as the Divine Demander, and do not force us to choose Your way, but demand that we make a choice in our will about Your Kingdom. Repentance means that we turn around completely from our old ways and embrace Your ways, Lord.

I face some more mystery. The Kingdom comes with an option to receive or deny it. Such is the parable of the mustard seed (Matthew13:31)—it's tiny and seemingly inconsequential, yet will one day be revealed as a massive tree and place of shelter and rest for many. So it will be at the coming of the Son of Man in glory—it is not about growth, but rather the mystery of the Kingdom. What is now seemingly small will—just like the mustard seed—swallow up this age, as the second coming of Christ reveals the incomparable, undeniable power of the age to come.

How humbling and terrifying that what we choose today has everlasting consequences that will affect us for all eternity. Christ demands a deeply thought out decision: that we will put Him first— before our families, ambitions, social lives or careers—and that we make choices with certainty, and consider the costly consequences of such action.

I am reminded of an old hymn, "As I survey the wondrous cross, on which the Prince of Glory died" and then the following lines, "Were the whole realm of nature mine, 'twould be an offering far too small...demands my soul, my life, my all." Do we see the demand? Do we bow to Christ and give Him all?

A Priestly Preparation

I am resolute that He will purify me and deal with my fears and insecurities. Lord, take away the distractions. Today, I feel flighty—I am in and out of Your presence, and do not quite manage to go deep enough to get a firm anchoring. Yet, suddenly You find me and take me into the inner recesses of intimacy with You. I am held. I realize that I have a strong will; it has been strong before in the wrong way (major stubbornness), but now, my Lord, my King, I am strong in You. My will is under Your Spirit, and I realize that. You have broken me before in this area, and I rejoice in fresh realization that my will is once again bowing to Yours. I am being tempered, and refined for my bridegroom King—it is a priestly preparation.

I do feel physically uncomfortable, but realize that leaving my comfort behind is a choice of worship. I worship and adore you, my sweet Savior.

Relinquishing Rights – Part of Cross Bearing

I have finally relinquished the vision for a "House of Prayer" in the region. I am learning to be a servant. I want to give ownership of everything to Christ. I am being emptied out—it was 85 percent joy and 15 percent pain to let it go. I sent the vision blueprint to some pastor friends. I gave them everything I have for the HOP vision, and explained that I wrote it a year ago and the reason for delay was partly God's timing and partly my pride in believing I could go it alone.

Ouch! I have no expectations. I have no presumption or assumption to a role, or if I am even to have no role. It is the Lord's and may His will be done. I have wrestled, prayed, wept and written many such blueprints for this house of prayer. I relinquish it in love, my dearest Friend. Be glorified. Release Your appointed ones to run with the vision. This is my gift to You and them. I give it up Lord. I am learning to be a blessing.

Lunchtime

I am being tested in the area of my temper. My youngest son, Samuel, went to bathroom on the carpet, instead of using the toilet! What a mess. Then, he scribbled on my bedroom wall with multi-colored crayons. This is so unlike him. I managed not to shout, and just quietly clean up the mess. If this had been some years before, I might have lost my temper, but You have taught me so much about being patient, Jesus.

Little by little, You are transforming my personality to be more like Yours. I muse on Your teaching about the law of anger (see Matthew 5:21-24). You are looking at the intent of our hearts, Lord. I see that murder is nothing but full-blown anger. An angry man, with a look that could kill, is as much in need of forgiveness as a murderer. May my actions reflect a pure heart, Lord. Purge me of my temper.

I am so tired—I have so little left to give my husband. Stephen is patient and gentle with me, and never pushes me beyond my limits. Thank you, Lord, that my husband is not demanding, and that he permits me to embrace You as my Husband and Maker in a new, deeper way without punishing me. Still, my desire is to be a loving wife. Father, grant me grace in this season to love in every way.

DAY 9 – Tuesday, November 9th

Fasting Knocks the Grumpiness Out of You!

I am irritable beyond words. I cried with the Lord, and asked Him to forgive me for being such a grumpy person. Today, I am Mrs. Grumpy with a capital "G." I cannot believe that I am in such a foul mood. I keep praying and asking for forgiveness. I am speaking to a youth group tonight, and I feel like a hypocrite. I spent the morning focusing on what I will be sharing about tonight—it's on the subject of prayer. I am preparing a visual display. God touches me with tenderness during this time.

I am truly blessed when Stephen and I pray together. He thanks You, Jesus, for the good fruit coming forth in me because of the fast. He prays for Your strength and encouragement for me. He was so delighted when I told him about giving away the vision for the house of prayer.

Samuel returns from nursery, and is so demanding today! He broke one of my good vases at lunchtime. Once again, I manage not to shout and just pick up the pieces. There are too many bits for me to glue it back together. I think about the Master Potter and the clay (see Jeremiah 18/19)—I need to be molded and shaped by the Potter today just to knock the grumpiness out of me!

I received a surprise check for $100—it was a gift from a lovely couple in America. Last week, a check for £50 arrived from a friend in Wales. Both of these are orders for the book I am writing. I am really encouraged. God keeps on doing this, and it is building my faith. I haven't even asked them for any money. It is totally a sovereign move of God.

Afternoon

I had an impromptu time together with two close friends, and received a beautiful single stem pink rose. I accept it from You, Lord. Each time I have done something significant for You these past few years, You have given me a single rose. I am deeply touched, because You give me a gift even in my grumpiness. This token reminds me that my security is found in Your love. There is nothing else that satisfies.

Beauty from Ashes

During the day, I noticed a small scrap of silver material lying on the floor. It belongs to Rebecca—I felt slightly annoyed that she had left it there on the floor. I saw it as nothing but a piece of rubbish to be thrown out. For some reason, I forgot to pick it up; I am so glad now that I did not. Later in the afternoon, Rebecca gave me a charming present—a tiny angel made from the scrap material, with a marble for the angel's head. I smiled, and then cried as You spoke to my heart with incredible tenderness: *"Child, that tiny scrap is just how I see humanity. I take what others would see as useless and only good to be discarded, and I transform them. I turn what is seen as rubbish into a thing of beauty and cause it to become a blessing. I see beauty where no one else does."*

The beauty of the Cross pounds my weary heart with exquisite precision, and fashions me to be something for Your Glory. I realize how much I have to learn, and I am grateful that You have given me a teachable spirit. I thank God for my petite daughter and her child-like faith, and ask, Lord, that You make me more like her. Compassion is growing in my heart. I see more clearly now that You perceive the potential of beauty in everyone, even in me when I am completely irritable. The power of Your blood to redeem mankind is remarkable Lord (see Revelations 1:5-6).

Evening

Tonight, we had fireworks. Samuel enjoyed them this year. I love the whizzing sounds and bursts of vibrant color. It was a special time, Lord—I forgot my irritability and had fun.

The youth meeting was excellent. Lots of unsaved kids, and some Christian children, attended and all responded well to the simple message on prayer. You supplied strength where I had none, and favor as well. Lord, how I bless You for your favor. I think of how You recently asked me to repent for unbelief in the area of favor, and I am grateful for the correction. I am walking in blessing, and not condemnation, and acknowledging Your provision of prosperity and providence.

Fasting is a Gift

In the evening, You explain to me that fasting is a gift. I am shocked. I had only seen it as a tool, and I often felt it to be a burden. *"Child, you have considered that fasting is a tool, and it has been a burden to you at times to carry. But, now see that I have given you this fast as a gift that you might know me more, and enter into the depths of intimacy with me. With the gift comes the grace. You have considered that this fast is your gift to me and, beloved child, I receive your gift of devotion and obedience. But my desire is that you understand that I have first given you the gift in order that you might return it to me as a love offering."*

How amazing, Lord, that You have given Your children such a gift. I am undone. I meditate on this gift for a long time. How foolish that I think it was my doing. All along, this has been from Jesus. My eyes begin to see more clearly. I see the beauty of fasting and set my face like flint to be God-reliant and not self-reliant, and to trust my Savior more fully.

DAY 10 – Wednesday, November 6th

In the middle of the night, I woke up to use the bathroom. I heard Your faint call to stay up. But I was horrible to You, Jesus. I said, "No way," and went back to bed. My irritability has lifted— it simply wasn't there when I woke up. God is so faithful. That truth is ringing loudly in my ears this morning. The Lord is asking me to focus on being a blessing and on giving rather than looking to receive or be blessed.

Fasting—A Choice for Jesus and Against the Flesh

I am ashamed to admit that I am somewhat materialistic. I hadn't realized that I had carnal desires in the area of possessions until starting this particular fast. With Christmas coming up, I am more aware of it. No more peeking at catalogs for the rest of this fast.

Head Lice and Housework

I met with a friend today. I wanted to be a blessing to her. I let her set the agenda for conversation. We spoke of head lice and housework. Although it was pleasant to see my friend, I found what we discussed to be somewhat strange. I am lovesick, Lord. I only want to speak of You, Jesus. Yet, I am so aware of Your love for everyone and to meet people right where they are at.

My friend shared some things with me that caused her to be vulnerable. I am able to hold my tongue. I share nothing with anyone. I am becoming more aware of the need to be particularly careful with words and how we speak of others. Conviction is increasing in this area, and the Lord is keeping a tight hold on me. I am grateful. I cover my sister, and do not allow the enemy to rob me of grace.

I came home, and found the energy to wash the kitchen floor, do some dusting and, generally, take care of a bit more housework. I am Mary in the midst of being Martha, and am contemplating You even as I work (see John 11). Thank You, Lord, for using my friend to inspire me.

DAY 11 – Thursday, November 7th

Crucifying the Language of 'I'

The mail arrives before Stephen and I have time to pray. The letters include a flier for a national "Leaders Together" training day. I would like to attend. I immediately begin to think of how I might manage to attend. Suddenly, I am convicted. My heart motivation is exposed before my King, and it is *not* attractive in His holy presence. Here I am again: I desire recognition with other leaders and, once more, I am led to repent. I feel convicted. I cry, because the desire is still there. Kingdom motivation is above any and all personal ambition. I surrender to Your will.

I am looking honestly at myself, and, quite frankly, I am struggling with this hidden place. I know the confinement is of You, Lord, and I understand it to be a deep refining and preparatory work. I comprehend in my head and my heart what it's all about, but I am still kicking and fighting. I've been here before, and I wonder how long I must stay in the place of preparation. Will I ever be ready? In this moment, the truth is that I am sick of the hidden place. How awful an admission, but it is the truth.

I want to be like the great evangelists and revivalist missionaries of old; I yearn to see countless souls saved and to move in miracles, signs and wonders. These are my daydreams and my prayers. These are the realities in which I long to live and breathe. Oh, the language of 'I' that must be crucified. In between my moaning, I repent. I cry out for the grace to stay hidden as long as it pleases You, Lord. Ultimately, I do grasp that preparation is necessary to carry responsibility for the times ahead.

When Stephen and I eventually pray together, we are both broken before Christ. Eventually, I end up interceding for sick people. So many people I know have cancer. Over the years, I have waged prayer wars against cancer for a number of people—I have such hatred for this disease. I recall in previous intercession, when I cried and screamed out to God, and begged Him for a miracle anointing to heal those who were suffering, in Jesus' name. I have wept and interceded to the point of utter exhaustion, where I can hardly whisper the name of my beloved Jesus. This morning, the Lord reminded me of these prayers: it is as if He is promising that the miracle anointing that I am asking for will indeed be mine in the fullness of time.

I am praying for a young man who has a brain tumor, as well as two other Christian male friends with prostate cancer. I think of another friend who lost his battle to cancer last year. I ponder on the brokenness in my heart regarding this. I am sowing, sowing, sowing and, one day, in Your grace, You will reap Lord. It's all for You, King Jesus.

Afternoon

Today, you gave me grace to give away the vision for the "Tartan Trucks" bus ministry. After meeting Bill Wilson (of Metro City Church, New York) in 1999, You birthed in my heart a vision for this bus ministry. A few weeks ago, I discovered that a nearby Christian fellowship has just begun a bus ministry that reaches out to children and young people. I was delighted and overjoyed.

Today, You told me to write to the pastor and pass on to him the vision blueprint You gave me. It is modeled on "Sidewalk Sunday School" with elements of William Booth's "jam- and-glory" salvation meetings: its ethos is to feed a hungry man, and then to share the gospel with him. Oh, Lord, I am rejoicing. This time of giving away was much easier than that of the house of prayer: 95 percent joy and only 5 percent pain! On Monday, we are meeting with the bus ministry pastor and his wife. Stephen has some ideas to help them with fund-raising.

I met for a planning/prayer meeting for "Change," which is our first ladies outreach night, to be on Wednesday, December 4th. It's only a few weeks away, but the venue is booked, the catering is sorted and my precious sister said "yes" to me yesterday. I am so excited that I can hardly wait.

Dining with the King

My friend gave me a handsome white and gold cup-and-saucer painted with a golden crown; it looks just like the one You gave me in the vision, Lord! It has a minute "number nine" painted on the base of the cup. I think of Your gifts and fruits, dear Spirit, and I am asking for all of them! (see Galatians 5:22-23; 1 Corinthians 12:7-11). I am dining with my King! I am the King's cupbearer.

I am learning to let You serve me, Jesus. Just the other day, I argued with You when You said, *"Child, you have never let me serve you."* That was until You gently reminded me of how You came as a servant king and also washed your disciples' feet. I am learning to receive Your abundance. I can only give away what I have received. I want to lavish Your love on the lost, Lord. I see Your banqueting table, and I want to bring the poorest-of-the-poor to eat there and partake of Your goodness. Lord, use our ladies outreach "Change."

The greatest blessing any person can know is fellowship with Christ. The Kingdom enters ours lives today through holy friendship with Jesus. The Bible teaches that this fellowship will be perfected in the Age to come—a time when we will be with God continually and see Him face-to-face (see Revelations 22:3-4). I can hardly wait, Lord.

I got lots done today. It was if I had supernatural speed! I did the fliers and the poem I will speak about at the ladies' night. My heart is to see lives transformed. "Change" is a combination of friendship and evangelism. Your Love has the right of way, Lord.

Evening

One of my spiritual daughters came by this evening. We cuddled up on the sofa and talked about You for most of the night. It was so lovely to spend time with her again. She is praying hard about her future and making plans for university. Grant her Your wisdom and counsel, Lord.

DAY 12 – Friday, November 8th

Last night, I had a dream that I woke up in the middle of the night and got up to pray. I remember, Lord, when You gave me grace to fast from sleep just after Samuel was born. I would stay up with You between the 2 a.m. and 6 a.m. feedings. These were glorious times, so filled with You. I catnapped during the day when Samuel slept. I was physically exhausted, but how my spirit soared! I don't have the same desire to get up and be with You Lord, and this is the second prompting this week. Please help me to obey.

I felt low when I got up, and had a real sense of heaviness on my spirit. The enemy's attacks are sometimes extremely subtle. I am barely awake when he begins with condemnation. I am almost too tired to argue, but I know that I must make a stand for truth. I quietly proclaim that "there is no condemnation for those who are in Christ Jesus" (Romans 8:1). I choose to praise You, Lord, and the heaviness begins to lift. I think about my conversation last night with my spiritual daughter, and I wonder about the wisdom in sharing my journey with her at this stage. Was my timing right? I'm not sure.

Brave Heart

We talked about the Brave Heart Conference, and I shared how You made a way for me to deliver a prophetic word for our nation. I am not sure she understood the process that I was trying to explain. I didn't mean to elevate myself, Lord. Please forgive me if I did. You are so faithful.

At this conference, it was a joy to hear Jack Deere teach on Scotland's prophetic heritage. When he prayed and asked You to release the prophets in Scotland, I thought I would just explode. At the beginning of the evening, I submitted the prophetic word You had given to me to leadership at the conference and, therefore, met protocol of respecting leadership. I really didn't mind who brought Your Word, just as long as it was spoken publicly.

Then right there, in a prayer pause pregnant with Kingdom destiny, You asked, *"If I asked you to go forward right now child, and it meant losing your reputation would you go?"* With all my heart I answered "Yes, Lord" (mostly, You have slain the monster of reputation within me). Then You told me I didn't have to go forward, and somehow I knew I had passed a test.

I closed my eyes and prayed, "Lord, You are sovereign. I believe in protocol. I have submitted this word, and I will not move unless You send someone for me." Seconds later, I opened my eyes, and then the evening's moderator asked me to go with him to the main stage and share the prophecy. I met Rick Joyner backstage, and he invited me to share the prophetic word. I was nervous. The cameras were rolling, but I just shut my eyes Lord and thought "it's just You and me, Jesus."

The people in the auditorium responded very well to the prophetic word. As I went to leave the platform, You reminded me of the vision I had that morning: I invited people to stand and then, as a person of Scottish descent, I prayed for the prophetic to be released in Scotland. So, I went back and asked Rick for the microphone once again. He graciously consented. I prayed, and a mighty wave of anointing broke loose from the back of the auditorium to the front.

You are awesome, Lord. I didn't even give my name—I wanted it to be a firstfruits offering for You, Lord. That night, I had been thanking You for a national platform. But, You corrected me and said, *"Child, I gave you a national platform at a leaders together gathering in the year 2000. This was an international platform."* I am still utterly amazed that You would use a broken vessel like me, Lord.

The Second Book

I started to type my diary entries today. Again, the enemy comes in like a flood. As I begin to type, it seems You are suggesting this will be my second book. (I find that to be quite funny: I haven't even finished the first one yet!) Immediately, the enemy comes in with accusation that I will lose my heavenly reward, because fasting is to be kept between me and my heavenly Father. If I go public, I will be a hypocrite who is working to impress man and is not worshipping God.

It is difficult to argue when he is quoting Scripture to me, but then Your gentle voice comes and I recognize Your authority, Lord. You tenderly share with me that You intend to use my journal as a way to encourage an army of believers to have a go at a 40-day fast. People are afraid of what they do not know. The honesty of my journey during this time, and its victory, will encourage many to try a longer fast.

Oh, Lord, I so want to believe that it is Your voice I am hearing, and that I am not justifying self-glorification. (I ponder the rest of my fast—in this moment, it does seem that I can make such an achievement. I think I might make the last week water only, and then on the last three days do not have any water or food. We will see.)

My editor has confirmed that he is coming from America, and is arriving around November 18th or 19th. I am so excited that we will get ahead with finishing the first book. Our friend from rehab is coming on the 22nd. Stephen's Alpha Course Holy Spirit weekend starts on the 23rd. Yikes, it is going to be crazy busy! I need to prepare sermons on "You are beautiful" (for next Tuesday) and "The Cross" (for next Sunday).

I managed to have a swim of about eight laps, and then took a whirlpool and a spa—all in 30 minutes. Then, I picked Samuel up from nursery. I am yearning for more time just to be with You, Jesus.

I just remembered another dream I had last night: it was a false representation of two dear brothers. Before I was even awake, the Holy Spirit broke in and explained, *"My child, this is how the enemy deceives my children and brings false accusation by giving false dreams that misrepresent other believers."*

Internal Ice Box

I am so cold. My teeth chatter, and my body shakes and shivers. I really feel like I am freezing. I am cold for the entire day. Maybe, it's just because I am fasting?

Afternoon/Evening

I went to a friend's place tonight to celebrate her daughter's birthday. I desperately wanted to eat some of their chilli con carne. Never has the smell of chilli wafted so sweetly up into my nostrils! As soon as I came home, I wanted to give up the fast. I lay on the bed thinking of my hunger, and asking You to fill me Jesus. Going back and forth in my emotions is a strong temptation to give up and give in. This morning, fasting for 40 days seemed so achievable. Tonight, that same amount of time now seems impossible. I am fidgety and I can't sit at peace.

DAY 13 – Saturday, November 10th

I spent some time lying in bed! I definitely feel brighter and more alert this morning than I have since I began fasting. This afternoon, I have yet another party to attend. It's more temptation to eat! I had fun being with the little ones as they partied. I got the opportunity to speak with the proprietor of the ceramic shop: she is a psychic and is deeply interested in spiritual matters. She asked my friend and I to return and have coffee with her, so that we could pray together. She seems so open. Lord, help us to harvest! (Also, I had my first bout of diarrhea. It was not nice.)

While reading the Bible, I am struck by Pilate's words, "What is truth?" (John 18:38) Lord, let Your truth rain down on me and let it reign through me. You are the Way, the Truth and the Life. Oh, Jesus, be the truth and the way for the dear psychic lady we just met. She is so confused and open to the counterfeit as well as the truth.

Later, I lie on my bed. I think of You Lord, and my heart is empty without Your manifest presence. I wonder why You seem so far away. I know that You beckon me to a deeper love, and this is the manner in which I enter in. Still, I feel as though my heart will break.

A Vision of the Bride – "You are Cherished"

I have a vision of once again being dressed as a bride. I was brought to my King in a horse-drawn carriage. A magnificent white horse with regal plumage carried me into Your courts. I felt so unworthy to be carried like this. You spoke simple words of love to me that are a salve my heart, *"I cherish you."* I lay down my doubts of being undeserving. You have another jewel for my crown! It's a gorgeous emerald. I ask, "What is the emerald for, Lord?" You reply, *"The emerald is my manifest presence."*

I cry a lot—it's silence and tears. I touch the empty space beside me on the bed. I want to see You there, Lord. I want to see Your face. I receive the gift with a grateful heart, but I still feel empty without You right here beside me.

I am sure other believers have also experienced this ache for greater intimacy with You, Jesus. You have no favorites, Lord, and cherish each one of us. Your desire is that every child of Yours would know how much You take pleasure in them, and also that they would experience the reality of Your manifest presence.

DAY 14 – Sunday, November 10th

I am amazed to think two weeks of my fast have passed. I am about one-third of the way there now.

Last night, the phone lines went down. Stephen is perturbed since British Telecom can't send someone to repair it until next Wednesday. They are rerouting our calls via my cell phone, but that doesn't help Stephen with the time he will miss from trading on-line. I believe You are speaking to my precious husband, Lord, and calling him to his destiny as a modern day Joseph. Maybe, this is the only way you can get his attention!

Passover and Intercession for the Heroin Addicts

Church is deep. As we walk into the building, I notice some discarded silver paper, a small plastic spoon and matches—all evidence of a poor soul's drug abuse from the night before. It was a cry for help! I am broken, and the anointing for intercession is like oil flowing down on my head. We worship, and I get an opportunity to share. Isaiah 53 is lifted up to You—we believe You will heal those washed out lives. I can hardly sing today. The weight of Your work of intercession rests heavily on me. I have no words, and only my lovesick heart. Two weeks left of fasting are nothing. How can I complain? Yet, in my weakness, I know I will do so again, but I am lost in the wonder of Your sacrifice.

I take communion and weep like a baby. I cannot hold back the floodgate of my tears as I think about the rivers of grace and mercy that flowed on the mount of crucifixion. I take the unleavened bread. I don't believe that doing this is breaking my fast. It's the first solid I've eaten in two weeks, but I couldn't neglect to honor and remember Your death on this Resurrection Sunday.

Precious Passover Lamb, we declare that Your arm was laid bare and won salvation for the nations. To those who pierce their arms with needles for the sake of heroin, we proclaim that they are healed by Your stripes. Come, Lord Jesus. These lives are not destined for the drain, but are destined to bring You glory. This morning, we are corporately convicted as a people. Bring in the lost souls that are starving for Your love and acceptance. We don't care about the smell, and we don't care about the inconvenience. Make us willing to love like You do. I can hardly hold back the scream, as I touch a tiny fragment of Your pain for these dear ones. Jesus, You wept.

Later On…

Stephen bought me a lovely bouquet of yellow roses, which are my favorite kind of roses. They remind me of being a bride. I feel Your hand on that gift Lord.

I spent this afternoon writing some cards and letters to bless other people, and it felt good. I prepared the Sunday dinner of roast chicken, vegetables, mashed potatoes and chicken gravy, finished off with trifle for dessert. The whole time was funny, because I ended up dipping my finger in the gravy boat. It tasted good, and I drank from it quite a lot! Once again, the kids were roaring with laughter, and Stephen just looked at me as though I had lost my marbles. Maybe I have!

CHAPTER 6

Week Three: The Gift of Tears

DAY 15 - Monday 11th November

Blistered Tonsils and Puddle Splashing

It's raining heavily today, and Stephen is stressed out because the telephone lines are still out of service. Rebecca is really ill, but I managed to get an emergency doctor appointment this morning. Unfortunately, it is at the same time that our pastor friends are due to arrive for morning coffee. I can't find their number. I can't find Stephen. I have tried four other friends, but no one answers.

I have no time—I need to take Rebecca to the doctor. Poor little girl is going to get soaked. But she never complains; she is such a blessing to me. We are seen quickly, and Rebecca gets penicillin for her blistered tonsils. We walk home again in the pouring rain, but we are laughing together in the huge puddles. The sky is grey, but we are still happy. Despite the enemy's relentless attempts to bring harassment, right now I feel impervious!

While at the doctor's office, I take the opportunity to ask him about long-term fasting. His response is quite positive, and he tells me to be careful when I end the fast to not eat any junk food or rush the process of re-establishing food intake. He says that I should expect to lose a pound a day as the fast progresses. I feel a bit freaked out by that information!

Stephen arrives home at the same time as we do. The pastors got the note I left them for them on the door, and they graciously waited for us to return. We have a lovely time together, and we just spend the time chatting and sharing honestly. They stay for lunch, and then two other friends turn up for an impromptu visit as well. We all sit around the table together, engage in some prayer time, and then everyone leaves just before I need to pick Daniel up from school. Oh, it's been such a busy day.

Later, as I process my thoughts, I feel Your gentle conviction, Lord. I am still prone to wanting to make a good impression. Forgive me, Father.

Hunger Hits Hard

It's dinner time and the hunger pangs have me hit HARD. I spend the rest of the night thinking about how hungry I feel. Usually, each day, there is perhaps an hour or so that I think a lot about food, but then it passes. Not tonight: I end up feeling depressed that all I can think about is food. The feeling doesn't go away. I snuggle up under a blanket and try to concentrate on the TV. I still feel really hungry and depressed that I can't have anything to eat for another four weeks. It doesn't seem possible. Will I have some toast? Oh, I long to eat. It's the worst evening I have had during the fast.

My left eye is droopy. My eyelid won't stop flickering—it's like a nervous tic, and it's really annoying. I look like the cartoon dog Droopy D! I am desperately tired, and I can't keep my eyes open. I go to bed feeling pretty miserable.

DAY 16 – Tuesday, November 12th

It's still raining heavily. Becca is still not well, and the medicine doesn't appear to be helping much. I'm still frantic for time alone with You, Lord, but my little one needs me. Please help me not to be irritable about a lack of private devotion time. It seems that the more I yearn to be alone with You, the more my time is taken. This is hurting my heart, Jesus.

I need to prepare my sermon for tonight. You have given me a word to share tonight on being beautiful! I did get the sermon done—it is tender and lovely, just like You, my Lord. Father, let there be a wonderful harvest tonight for Your glory.

Prayer – A Choice

I try to pray for the meeting tonight. I want to cry. It's lunchtime. I feel so alone. Prayer is difficult today, there is no comfort and every word is an effort. It's a choice to pray, but I feel lacking in the Spirit's sovereign guiding. Why are You silent? Is there a blockage? I'm disappearing; I feel bland and empty. In this place of perceived abandonment, I start to weep. Where are You, Lord? Where are You? I know You are near, but where are You?

It's a relief to let the tears fall. I need the release. What are they? Tears of longing, frustration or even self-pity? Not at all, in this moment they are for You, my Lord. Please come, Lord, and visit with me. Fill the aching longing in my heart. I feel small and childlike. I call out Your name: Jesus, Jesus, Jesus. I remind myself of Your many words to the Bride in Song of Songs. I still don't feel any consolation. I want YOU!

Stephen comes home for lunch, and asks me why I am crying. I don't want to have to explain my tears. He asks me, "What was it you expected from your fast?" It's not a one-word answer. I don't want to speak. I don't mean to exclude him, and I am not trying to be superior. I'm in the middle of the pain, and I can't articulate it without it sounding inaccessible to another. I don't mean to be unkind. I believe I understand the process that I am going through. I have been here before, but never in this depth. It's just so hard. The anguish to be fully one with Christ is deeper than I've ever known. My answer to Stephen's question is: "I guess I expected more highs than lows." Somehow the lows are outweighing the highs, but, I thank You,

Lord, for the wondrous highs when they come. Is it normal to have more lows than highs?

I have a bowl of carrot soup. It has stopped raining. Now there is stillness in my soul. The raw emotion begins to be blotted out as Your perfect peace saturates my being. I feel the increase. Now that I am calm again, I am able to carry on. My mind is quiet now. Peace at last.

Not for long! The devil tries to convince me that You were ignoring me. That's not true. He's a liar and a thief. I will not let him rob me of Your peace.

I think about ordering some Christmas presents for Daniel. I know I will feel much better if I do because I love to bless. But I remember what I promised myself: no catalogs. Instead, I'll quietly wait on You, Lord. I am tired now, in a rested sort of way. I'd like to sleep and dream of You, but the children need my attention. I think about baking but quickly dismiss the thought. I don't think I could endure the delicious aroma of cakes and cookies baking in the oven. I realize that even when all I have to offer You are my tears, they are enough.

The afternoon passes, and I make the evening meal and then prepare to leave for the meeting. My friend and I share some lovely prayer and worship in the car. There are only about a dozen or so women at the meeting, but those who came are blessed by the sensitive word on Your beauty, Lord, and their loveliness in You. This is the shortest sermon I have ever preached. It's a simple message, and I didn't feel particularly anointed, Lord. I hope and pray that this is part of what You are doing. It's not about what we "feel," but what we know to be true by Your Spirit. It's a torrential downpour of rain all the way home. Thank You, Jesus, for journey mercies.

DAY 17 – Wednesday, November 13th

Rebecca is still not going to school. Now, her poor tongue is covered in blisters, her tonsils are full of poison and her glands are swelling up! We go off to the doctor's office once more. A swab sample of her mouth is taken to test for bacteria, and then we return home. It's more torrential rain, but at least today we have the car.

The phones are finally fixed. Yeah! Stephen can get back to Internet sales, and I can make phone calls again. I received an e-mail from a colleague inviting me to their next house of prayer meeting. I wonder why none of the men have responded yet to the vision I sent them? It's weird. I'm trying not to get in the flesh Lord, but it's not easy. Why has no one acknowledged that they have received it? I thought it was a beautiful gift, but only silence comes as a response. I just don't get it, but I'll wait patiently for the answer.

I've Lost 12 Pounds!

This afternoon, I went to visit my sister. I weighed myself on her bathroom scale and was astonished to find I've lost 12 pounds in the short space of time I've been fasting. I didn't think I would lose that much weight. I am a bit worried about how much more I might lose before the end of the fast.

I was horrible and lost my temper with Samuel when he had an accident at my sister's. His poop was everywhere: all over his legs and bottom, the toilet, and the floor. Oh, I just wasn't in the mood for it today, Lord. I ended up yelling, even though I knew I made a completely wrong response for a little boy learning to be potty-trained. We had just gotten Samuel all cleaned up when he wet himself again and needed a further change of clothes. He simply forgot to look where he was sitting and his urine spilled over. Oh well, at least this time it was only pee.

Dinner was a war zone. I am tired of my oldest son not eating. He hates *everything* I cook. It is difficult not to get angry with him when he sits at the table night after night and complains about his food, eats a few mouthfuls and then follows with a sullen, sulking refusal to eat. I am weary of it. I ended up shouting at him. He was in tears. I wanted to cry also, but I shouted instead. I felt awful, yet I am at the end of my rope with him. Normally, I wouldn't bother, but with the fast and my sitting at the table and not eating, everything to do with food seems exaggerated. Stephen is upset about it all too. What is the answer Lord?

Terrible Parent Syndrome

I go to my room, lie on my bed and cry. For a short time, I suffer from "I am a terrible parent" syndrome as I think of how I've reduced two of my precious children to tears today. I hate the fact that I did so. I feel ashamed at my lack of effective parenting. Then, I hear Your voice Lord, *"Child, open your heart and let my peace come in."*

But I am too angry: I can't yield. Instead, I settle for a horrible cloak of shame. In this moment, I detest this fast because I feel so miserable today. Is it just a glorified diet, because my behavior seems to have gotten worse? What is happening to me? I am fed up with not eating, and I am feeling very sorry for myself and hurt inside. I look at my heart with loathing. Lord, help me to love myself.

The phone rings, and I speak with my fasting buddy. I complain and then feel a little bit better. She's had a rotten time, too. Her vacuum cleaner blew up, her washing machine has gone on the blink, and her little boy got hit on his hand by another child and had to go to the doctor's office with a bruised, swollen limb! She feels tearful and crabby, too. We remind each other that this fast is a gift. It's by Your grace Jesus that we stand.

I go for a bath and You call to me again, *"Child, open your heart and receive my peace."* I say, *"I can't Lord"* and you reply, *"Yes you can. Lay down the cloak of shame you have chosen to wear and yield to my love."* I make a Spirit-led choice, and begin to experience the warmth of Your Father's love—I feel it intensely.

A Vision of the Ancient of Days

I have a vision: I am lifted in the Spirit, and see myself falling at Your feet and grabbing a hold of Your ankles. You are seated on Your throne, and You look like the Ancient of Days. I am fascinated and embraced in this awesome love of my Dad! You lift me from Your feet, and sit me on Your knee. You say, "Look into my eyes child." Then, You begin to croon a lullaby to me, *"Hush little baby don't you cry."*

Great fat rolling tears run down my cheeks. I don't deserve this perfect love, but I receive it. I look into your eyes, which are blazing like fire, and I see Jesus on the Cross. I realize that I am not perfect, but we don't have to be perfect in ourselves: You made us perfect in You at the Cross of Calvary. I rest. Your hair is white and Your eyes shine as You hold me close. I release more healing tears and then fall into peace.

Tonight, Stephen received an e-mail from a Christian fund-raising organization in London, and they want him to fly down for a business meeting as soon as possible. They are excited about his ideas. He only sent the letter yesterday, and they already prayed and e-mailed him back. Stephen and I are both thrilled.

Another Vision – the Joseph Anointing

I have another vision: I see Stephen flying into his Kingdom destiny. It's so quick, it's a "suddenly." I see him in offices and appointing staff, and it's huge undertaking. It's the Joseph anointing beginning to flow into the nations. Oh, bless You, Jesus. I enter the vision, and then I discern the accusing adversary moving into this spiritual realm. In the vision, my hands are bound and then a muzzle is placed over my mouth. I am receding into the background. The accuser whispers to me, "Your ministry is over when Stephen's begins."

I simply rest in Your sovereignty Lord, because I know the devil is a liar and a thief. I pray, "Prosper him, Jesus, prosper him. I give up everything that another might be served." The accuser disappears, and I know a deep inner peace. I will not be silenced or muzzled by the enemy. Not my will be done, but Yours Lord.

My stomach rumbles all night. I have a can of aerated juice and momentarily enjoy the sugar rush. But it doesn't help—I still feel hungry, and now slightly sick. I try to remind myself that this is only for a season—it won't always feel this uncomfortable. I still want those miracles.

Late at night, a pastor calls. He asks me what I will preach on this Sunday, and, immediately, I feel that I should speak on Isaiah 53, the Cross and healing. I go to bed with Isaiah 53 beginning to open up to me. Healing belongs to us because it belongs to you—it's covenant healing. I am embedded in You, Jesus. You engraved me on the palms of Your hands. I am Your Bride. We will be made spotless because of Your blood.

DAY 18 – Thursday, November 14th

I feel much calmer this morning than I did yesterday. The kids are all on vacation from school until Tuesday. Grant me grace, Lord. I receive a really difficult e-mail from a close friend, which carried a rebuke that I don't believe was merited. I have e-mailed him back and tried to be humble and gentle, but honest. Lord, why now? I believe Your love will heal all.

Mark is still sulking. The other kids have been well behaved this morning. They are playing happily together and not fighting. Thank You, Jesus. The morning has sped by and nothing untoward happened, with the exception of receiving my friend's e-mail. But he has sent me another message and everything is fine. Thank You, Jesus.

The children play well: Daniel's friend comes round to play; and now Mark is coming out of his mood now. I get lots of paperwork done, both for the household and the ministry. Tidying up administration is an important task. I don't like it much, but it is necessary. I managed to secure a date for our next meeting for "Move" in Ireland. "Move" is a vision to mobilize children and young people to have a conference "on the move," and to travel to various locations within the United Kingdom. Everyone is free on December 12th, so we'll stick with that date.

My tongue is disgusting. I mean the actual physical tongue is like a fur ball. My teeth have felt disgusting since day one! It's as if I have constant bits of fuzz growing in them. No matter how I brush my teeth, my tongue has this weird coating. How revolting!

Evening

In the evening, another of my spiritual daughters arrives. My concentration is bouncing all over the place. I had forgotten that she was coming. We have such a precious time together. We talk about Teen Challenge and their bus ministry. I would like to help, Lord, but I wonder if I am totally out of line to consider this when I've just given away the ministry vision for "Tartan Trucks." It's working with addicts, alcoholics, street girls, and homeless people. Perhaps You will graciously permit me to go? My young friend shares her heart and her dreams. Oh, Lord, You are glorious—she has found her niche! Just after she leaves, I call her brother. How I love his poetic, worshipping heart. (I've had no time to write the sermon for Sunday yet, but ideas are beginning to form.)

DAY 19 – Friday, November 15th

I get up and stare out the kitchen window at the little cherry blossom tree—it's now so stark and vulnerable without leaves or blossoms. Earlier in the week, I noticed that it had only a few leaves remaining. Looking at it made me think of myself being pruned and stripped away. Today, the tree is totally bare. Strong winter winds have forced it to give up its final covering. A squall of wind lifts up its last three remaining golden leaves and carries them away. I feel like that tree; I am bare before You, Lord. This is winter, but I know that spring will surely come at the appointed time. Thank You for the seasons, Lord, and the law of the harvest, which is simply this: a seed will bear fruit at the appointed time, when it is planted and nurtured.

You remind me, Lord, that You were pruned by Your Father. The Bible says that every branch that did not bear fruit was taken away, and every fruit-bearing branch was pruned to make it more fruitful (see John 15:1-2). Thank You, Lord, that You have gone before us, and that You completely empathize and understand where we are at and what we are experiencing. Pruning is about paring away what would prevent growth. Spiritual pruning is surrendering to your love-filled discipline in our lives. If it's good enough for You Lord, then it's good enough for us.

I am so hungry this morning. I got up and managed to write the sermon draft in just an hour and a half. It is awesome, Jesus. Please, Lord, I ask You to heal many on Sunday through this word.

I am trying to arrange to meet up with some friends from America during their trip to United Kingdom in December. I need to take the kids out—the house feels as though it is shrinking! At lunchtime, I was so tempted by the smell of sausage rolls. Never have they smelled so delicious! Stephen said, "You're almost half way now. You could just do a 20-day fast." I replied, "I could, but then that would only be half of what God asked me to do."

A Vision of Beautiful Blooms—Joy at Last!

I decided to take the children to an indoor play park during the afternoon. During the drive, I listened to some worship music and had an open vision of You, Lord. I could see You as You were smiling at me. You spoke, *"I am inviting you to walk with me child."* I saw myself dancing in the vision, and incredible joy burst forth in my spirit. Oh, at last, a feeling of joy! I saw flowers all along the pathway You called me to walk on; they are beautiful blooms that will last for all eternity. They speak to me of being fruitful in the Kingdom.

I met a friend at the indoor play park. Our kids ran off to climb and swing on the ropes, and we sat down to enjoy a cup of coffee. We spoke of learning to be more dependent on You. Independence is a sin because it is rooted in pride and self. While chatting, we discerned two drug dealers right in the middle of the children's indoor play park. We prayed, and also spoke to the management there. Lord, let Your light shine into the darkness.

Just before we arrived at McDonald's, You spoke again to my heart Lord: *"I have called you to a 40-day fast, not 20. You can do it. You have grace enough for another 20 days. I didn't create you to be one who gives up half way. I created you to be full and overflowing. It is necessary that you fast for 40 days. You can do it."* The prophet Daniel fasted for 21 days, and that was enough for him. Could that not be enough for me? I hear a resounding "no." I wonder why, but no answer comes. Jesus, it isn't easy when You seem to ignore me, but it causes me to want to persevere for Your mercy filled answer. Your grace is sufficient for all our needs.

Being at McDonald's with Stephen and the children was agony. I don't think I can do that again. The smell of all the food was making me feel ravenous. Why am I so weak-willed? Why am I still hungry? Will it ever stop?

On the way home, I was lifted into Your presence, Lord. You were giving me a third stone—it was amber. I asked You what that means, and You replied, *"Amber is for resilience and speaks of your burning devotion for your King."* Just as I returned to full consciousness of my physical surroundings, we pulled up to a set of traffic lights. A billboard loudly announced, "You can have what you want, when you want it." I am struck that this so contradicts Your way, my Lord. I want to live my life doing and saying what You want, and not what I want. How You love when Your children are devoted to You alone.

Evening

In the evening, I went out to a jewelry party. More food brought me more agony. At a table in front of me sat all of my favorite snacks. I held my mug of coffee, and pressed in for Your strength. I was astonished at the deep desire I had to jump the tables and ram food into my mouth. You steadied me. I left after two long hours, and, rather selfishly, thought how unfair it was that others could eat while I could not. I'm at home and my stomach rumbles like nothing on earth. I go to bed hungry and tired.

DAY 20 – Saturday, November 16th

I didn't sleep well: I had a horrible nightmare. However, I woke up to the sound of loud cheering from Heaven. I ask the Lord what it was: He showed me a picture of the great cloud of witnesses and of angels, who were all clapping and cheering because I had made it halfway through my fast. I was startled and overwhelmed that a woman in Scotland would be of any significance to the cloud of witnesses, yet I was reminded of Hebrews 2 and how saints of old love to encourage today's saints to more great works for Christ.

The Vision of the Tree

Then, I had a vision of myself standing on a tree. Two branches were before me: one was quite wide and, therefore, easy to walk on; the other was extremely narrow and looked difficult to scale. I decided the narrow branch was the best way to go. I walked along it intrepidly. Holding out my arms to balance myself, I made a tightrope journey to slowly inch towards the end of the branch. Near the last part of the branch, I found myself on my hands and knees, clinging on for dear life. Finally, I was able to edge myself to the very tip of the branch—that's where I began to eat the beautiful fruit growing there.

Then, suddenly You appeared sitting with me on the branch, Lord. I believe that this vision speaks of the next 20 days. The first half of my journey is over, but the second (and perhaps more difficult part) may well have to be done in an even more God-reliant way. I desire to cling to You, Lord—it is necessary or I will fall. I want to partake of the beautiful fruit you have shown me, but it can only come through humble obedience in this journey.

Now that I am up, I typed my sermon for tomorrow. This afternoon, we are going swimming with the children, so that will be fun. I want to find some quality prayer time today. Please help me, Lord, not to be complacent and give up at 21 days! I am still hungry, and my stomach continues to rumble more so than in the beginning. That's quite strange. I feel as if my gums are shrinking along with my waistline. Feeling your gums receding from your teeth is a very funny sensation.

I went up to the village to High Street to do some shopping because I needed some greetings cards. I bought some stocking fillers, and then ended up in the second-hand shop. I bought two beautiful outfits for the princely sum of £17! What a bargain. I actually went in to purchase a little tea set for Samuel's Christmas stocking, but then a few other items of clothing caught my eye. I tried them on—I cannot believe a size 10 almost fits me again. It's been years (well, at least three babies ago) since a size 10 could even come close to fitting me!

The outfits are gorgeous. One is a hand-beaded, long silk skirt, with cream georgette and satin camisole top decorated with tiny beads and sequins, and finished off with a grey velour bolero—it is a truly stunning outfit. The other ensemble is a black beaded skirt with a midnight blue Chinese-style top, also in velour and decorated with fine silver embroidery detail. I even managed to pick up a lovely black velvet skirt for Rebecca. I feel like a princess in my new clothes. I love rummaging around in the "junk" and discovering beautiful things!

I came home and, for a second, I panicked; I thought that I had broken my agreement with You, Lord, to bless others before I bless myself. But You speak tenderly to my heart, *"Child, today you felt like a princess and that is what I want you to feel like, because that, my darling, is what you are to Me— My beautiful bride."*

I haven't felt good about myself for most of this fast, but I feel good today. A deep reservoir of joy is beginning to open up to me. But this joy isn't just for me—it's for all Your children. We are all Your children and, therefore, Your heirs. We have a royal inheritance! This place of acceptance is a haven of prayer, and is drenched in Your peace, my beloved Bridegroom King. You long for Your Church, Your Bride, to know the depth of Your Bridegroom love. Father, I ask You to birth awareness in Your children to embrace the reality of their Kingdom inheritance.

I had fun planning Rebecca's upcoming 7th birthday party. We've decided to have it at home with a company that does princess dress-ups, with make-up, a craft activity and a photo included. The event sounds like "girlie heaven" and Rebecca loves the idea.

Afternoon

The sports center was fun. While I was in the swimming pool, Lord, You asked me a question: *"If I told you that the discomfort you endure today will one day bring comfort to others, would you continue in your discomfort? Will you love them more than you love yourself?"* My answer was a resounding "yes." You speak to me of the nations that are Your inheritance. There is nowhere on earth we can set our feet that is not already given by the Father (see Psalm 2:8). My Lord, teach us how to be Your Kingdom ambassadors on the earth, to put You first and to love others as we love ourselves.

We all enjoyed our swim. It was a shame that Daniel and Mark had a bit of a fight in the changing room, which ended with Mark's T-shirt being stolen by another boy! Oh, Lord, if the little boy needed it then bless him, but show him that stealing is wrong.

We had a Chinese take-out meal for dinner. I didn't sit at the table tonight; instead, I enjoyed a wonderful time of intercession with my Lord. After the last delicious remains of stir-fried chicken and rice was gone, I joined my family for a warm milky drink.

Evening – Learning to Love like Jesus

I attended a prayer and praise meeting in the local church—it is an attempt to get the region praying and worshipping together. The gathering was small, but several different denominations were represented. I knew all of the other leaders, which was a delight. One of the pastors shared that God wanted to teach us how to love, and, as he told us this, I saw a picture of Jesus weeping tears of joy. His intercession spilled over onto my cheeks, and I sat in the pews and wept silently as I heard the Spirit speak, *"I have waited such a long time for my children to love like this."* This time together was deep and moving, and I was blessed to witness this new stirring for unity and love within the body of Christ in our region.

I returned home, and watched a documentary about soccer hooligans. Looking at such anarchy was simply shocking. I wonder if these poor, wretched souls will ever know Your compassion. My Lord, save them from violence and wickedness.

I feel exceedingly unwell tonight. It is as if I am freezing internally—I shake a lot and it doesn't feel good. I've noticed the cold feeling increasing this last week. No amount of extra layers of warm clothes helps. I am also extremely nauseous this evening. My stomach is painful, too.

DAY 21 - Sunday, November 17th

Two Pairs of Pajamas, a Wet Bed and a Sermon

We had an absolutely awful night with Samuel. He was up and down all through the night. He wet himself twice, and one of those times was in our bed at 6 a.m. I was grumpy, tired and extremely irritated. I was angry and directed it towards You, Lord: I asked why You were allowing this to happen and stated that I would be too tired to preach. After stripping the bed and changing Samuel into dry pajamas, my head hit the pillow and, before I fell asleep, I whispered prayers of repentance for my grumbling, hard-hearted attitude.

I almost slept in too late for my speaking engagement! I woke up at 9 a.m. with only 45 minutes to wash my hair, tidy up and get ready. I left the house with piles of unwashed laundry, and I kissed Stephen and told him that I would attend to it when I returned. I cried when we arrived at the church. We had a quiet time to pray for 30 minutes before service. As we prayed, I felt restored by Your peace. Your presence settled like a mighty cloak upon me. Thank

You, Father, that You are faithful even when I am faithless. I am glad You are on Your throne, my Lord and King.

The meeting was awesome. A believer sang and played her bugle as a powerful prophetic action and a wake-up call to the Church. The worship was delightful, and then, Lord, I found it so easy to preach Your word on healing and the Cross. I was just lost in Your embrace. The prophetic flow was magnificent. Glory to Your name! After the meeting, we went on to fellowship with the people from church. At lunch, You provided the most scrumptious homemade soup with no lumps! Thank You, Jesus, for these dear people.

I returned home around 3.45 p.m. I kissed my kids, hugged my husband and went to work on that laundry! Then, I prepared the dinner, served it, made up the beds and then collapsed in a heap around 7.30 p.m.

Rapid Weight Loss

I weighed myself again today. Only three weeks ago, I weighed in at 146 pounds. Last Tuesday, I weighed in at 132 pounds and today, only five days later, I am at 124 pounds. To be honest, I am alarmed at the sheer speed that the weight is falling off of me. I am not in fear, but I am a bit anxious. In three weeks, I have lost almost 22 pounds. I have a cut off point in my mind; I don't want to go below 112 pounds. I need to believe, Lord that, in faith, You will not let me lose any more weight once I reach this mark.

I am extremely tired and want to sleep. I think Stephen feels excluded. I bark at him (so unfair of me), and we fall asleep in a slightly-hurt-but-hugging-each-other way.

Chapter 7

Week Four: 'Sorry' and a Tin of Soup

DAY 22 – Monday, November 18th

I received an Internet order today for two more copies of my unfinished first book, *The Normal, the Deep and the Crazy*. My boys are extremely boisterous today. Mark has just broken Rebecca's plastic shovel, which she is extremely upset about. I believe it was an accident but, nonetheless, it was unnecessary. I don't have the energy to deal with harassment again today, Lord. Please intervene. I am leaving in a few moments to take Mark to the orthodontist. At least, that should break up the bickering for a little while.

The journey to the orthodontist was terrible! Mark spent most of the time slapping Daniel on the head through the back of the seat—I found it distracting to drive with the ever-increasing noise level. We arrived at the orthodontist, and Mark was very brave having the anchor fitted to his back teeth. The kids asked if we could go to McDonald's, but I couldn't face it. They moaned, and I felt guilty.

Rebecca gives Daniel a Punch!

I decided to go to the Christian bookstore, and I look for a small teddy keepsake gift for the psychic lady I met recently. The kids stayed in the car while I headed into the store. Unfortunately, only one staff member was on duty because it was lunchtime. So, it took me 10 minutes to make my purchase, which was twice as long as I had expected. I returned to the car to find Rebecca and Daniel in floods of tears! Rebecca had punched Daniel! I can hardly believe it—it is so out of character for her to do anything like that. How can all hell break loose in such a short space of time? Apparently, Daniel was teasing her, and she lost her cool and swung at him. They both apologized to each other, and then we were able to get on our way. Oh dear, this is hard work today.

On the return journey, I noticed another billboard: it had a picture of four fishermen holding a huge fish. The caption on the board read, "Together we are stronger." I agree, Lord. Father, Son, Holy Spirit and me—together we are stronger. I can do nothing without you. The image of the fishermen speaks to me of the coming end time harvest. I long to be used by You as a harvester, Lord.

Shaking, Shivers & Dizzy Spells

I feel physically unwell again today. I am exhausted, and it's difficult to find energy to talk, let alone move! I experience those internal shivers and feel like I am losing my battle to fast. I want to eat. I am dizzy and the room is spinning all over the place. My clothes are falling off of me. I have one pair of trousers that fit, but even they fall down: I have to keep pulling them up to maintain my dignity.

Breakdown and a Piece of Toast

Dinnertime comes, and exhaustion is overtaking me. I feel as if I cannot go on. I need to eat—I decide that I am going to. I make myself a piece of toast, and sit down with my family and eat it. It feels so strange to chew after 22 days of not doing so. I feel slightly sick as the bread gets digested. It's almost too big an effort to eat the simple bread. I am so sorry, Lord, but I need to eat—I can't go on without food.

I clear up the dishes and feelings of total failure begin to engulf me. I am resolute that I am going to complete these 40 days with You, but I simply have to add a piece of bread to my diet. My lifestyle is too hectic. I can't lie down when I feel exhausted. I want to be obedient, but I also feel that I cannot cope with the strenuous demands of being a busy wife, a mother to four lovely children and also a minister of the gospel. It's too much to do, Jesus, without any food. I am so sorry.

The phone rings: two friends call, one after another. Despite my sense of dismal failure, laughter breaks out from somewhere deep within me. I tell my friend about the fast and ask him to pray for me. Perhaps some more prayer will help me to complete the 40 days? Quite unexpectedly, my friend begins to prophesy on the telephone, and says that my fast will become material for a book. Wow! What a confirmation Lord of what You have secretly spoken to my heart. What incredible timing that I should receive this word from You while I am at such a low ebb. You are so kind to bless me with Your abundant love.

'Sorry' and a Tin of Soup

But these kind words aren't enough to distract me from my horrible hunger pangs. I am still starving. I go to the shops and buy a can of soup broth. Coming home, I whisper, "Sorry, sorry, sorry" all the way. My heart is aching as I open the can of soup. I sit down to eat it with a second piece of bread, and tears cascade down my cheeks. I swallow gulps of delicious vegetables and bread, but my heart is breaking and I weep and weep. Swallowing like this is not easy. Forgive me, Lord.

The enemy comes in like a flood. He reminds me of the vision of the tree and its fruit. I see myself on that tree, and several demons around me are kicking, punching and trying to throw me off. I know this is not from You, Jesus, and I reject it in your mighty Name.

I ask You for grace and resilience to continue to the end of the 40 days, even if it means adding a slice or two of bread each day, and perhaps the odd bowl of soup with lumps! This is still a thing of beauty in Your eyes—I am not a failure. (Now that I have eaten, the physical shaking has stopped—that is a relief.)

This evening, I am re-reading Rees Howell's *Intercessor*, and it speaks volumes to me. I understand that so much of this journey has been in the dealing of "self" more than "sin." As the purity of the Divine Person of the Holy Spirit draws ever nearer to me, I am convicted in the area of "self." You call us to surrender and sacrifice, which is much more than mere service. I understand that, Lord. I am keenly aware that surrender has multiple levels. Surrendering to Your ways is one matter, but it's quite another to allow the Holy Spirit to live His life completely through me. Yet, I want to yield to You completely, Lord. I see that much more decrease is required so that You may increase. Oh, come, Precious Spirit, and have Your way. I fall asleep in Your arms.

DAY 23 – Tuesday, November 19th

I wake up and wonder about the future. I think of Psalm 2:8, "Ask of me, and I will make the nations your inheritance, the ends of the earth your possession." This is Your inheritance Lord, and, therefore, it is also the inheritance of Your Church. Love for the nations burns brightly in my heart.

The children return to school, and I note that my resolve to fast is still intact. Hallelujah! I skip breakfast—as has been my routine since beginning my fast—and then Stephen and I have our typical morning prayer time. I then enjoy a lovely time of prayer and fellowship—just You and me, Jesus. I haven't recorded all my prayer times during these last few weeks, but that doesn't matter.

A friend comes by for coffee and to catch up. We are discussing the possibility of working together in early December, when he is hosting a worship team from Brazil. We're planning to organize a visit to a ravaged housing estate in a nearby town. The trip will be for the purpose of worship and dance in the streets, and we believe it will usher Jesus' presence into this needy place of such hurting souls.

DAY 24 – Wednesday, November 20th

Silence—the air is full of silence. I miss Your voice, and long for You speak to me again, but instead, but its only silence. The empty spaces are filled with searching and questions.

As I am driving to pick my editor up for our appointment, You speak to my heart. Oh, glory, I didn't have to wait long at all for Your tender call. In a vision, I see You holding something in Your hand. You smile at me, and open Your palm to reveal a beautiful sapphire. I ask what it is for, and You chuckle and say, *"It's for you. The sapphire speaks of the firm foundation you have found anchored in Me and represents the path that leads into my presence."*

I think of Moses and the elders who walked the sapphire path of your presence (see Exodus 24:9-10). How You love to invite Your children into the depths of intimacy with You, Lord. Only through royal relationship with You can Your bride usher in Your dominion rule on the earth.

I pick my editor up at 9:30 a.m. for our first meeting. He is a lovely man. We go to a regional prayer gathering and pray and worship together. The team discusses the blueprints I sent them for the house of prayer. Despite my initial puzzlement over no one responding, they are all delighted; they think that my plans are well thought out and can be multiplied in any area. Hallelujah! I'm glad You helped me to be patient and not to presume rejection.

Later, while praying in the sanctuary, my heart is ripped wide open with Your pain. The Holy Spirit and a deep travailing prayer breaks upon us. We weep and intercede in a posture of humility and repentance. We worship some more, and then the pastors re-dedicate the church to you, Lord.

Returning home, Stephen meets with my editor, and we spend the day chatting together, sharing a meal (I had a slice of toast) and finishing up at around 10:30 p.m. I am totally exhausted. It's been blessed, but also extremely intense. I am tired from all the talking, of which I did a huge amount.

DAY 25 - Thursday, November 21st

When I went to bed last night, I felt exceptionally tired. However, when I awoke early this morning, I was refreshed and my thoughts were full of You, dear Jesus. I think about yesterday, and how spent I felt by the end of the day. You remind me that this fast is necessary, and I feel a new surge of Your resolve and strength. I don't think I could make it through the next three weeks of editing the book without Your strength. Please grant me grace, patience, wisdom and humility, Lord.

Today, I just need to "be." I drive for miles without any music playing, and just enjoy the Jesus-filled silence that my soul and spirit are so desperate for today. I don't ask You for anything; I just want to spend time with You, Lord. It's been too busy—too many voices, too much to say and do. Now, it's just You and me and it's bliss.

Much later, I go Christmas shopping and buy lots of little odds and ends. A close companion of mine pops by, and we have a coffee and prayer time. I'm scheduled to see my editor tomorrow, and we also have another friend from rehab arriving at some point during the day. Stephen is teaching at the Alpha course tonight. Bless him, Lord.

Evening

It's a challenging evening! The telephone rings non-stop, which is difficult with four children around and only one adult. Samuel has another accident, and I have to clean up a whole mess of poop. I finally sit down at 9:40 p.m. No sooner do I rest my weary limbs that I manage to knock over a whole pint of juice onto the carpet! On reflection, this may be a blessing in disguise since the glass contained lemon juice and orange juice, which is possibly not the kindest refreshment during a fast!

DAY 26 – Friday, November 22nd

I rise early once more, and spend solitary moments in silent prayer and contemplation—it's a balm to my soul. The first image I see when opening my eyes is a phrase in my mind: "Catherine Who..." I laugh out loud, and wonder if that's the title for my book. Perhaps, it is more about understanding that my identity is to be found in Christ alone.

It's 9:15 a.m., and I drop off Samuel at nursery school. My head is full of John 5 and the Biblical truths contained in it. Yesterday, during my Biblical meditation, the whole chapter began to open up to me in a fresh revelatory way. As soon as I woke up this morning, I made some notes on the passage.

I went to the supermarket 15 minutes after dropping Samuel off at nursery school. I do some speedy shopping, and my editor arrives at the supermarket to meet me. I feel tired and weepy now. My period is due tomorrow—perhaps that's why I feel the way I do? Hormones! Who would have them?!

On the drive home, we pass by some 15 firemen on strike from work. They are part of a national strike initiative, which hopes to secure a substantial pay raise for all firefighters in the United Kingdom. I feel the nudge of the Holy Spirit to encourage them. So, I pull over and, with biscuits in hand, offer them a coffee time treat, and thank them for all their hard work and devotion. They seem genuinely blessed that I took the time to do so.

Back home with the shopping unpacked, my editor and I continue to share some life stories and testimonies. I have a further vision, which speaks of the book: I see a picture of myself laughing on a book cover with the caption, "Who is this woman!?" Lord, we need Your help to edit the manuscript. Please lead and instruct us.

Fixing lunch for the men quickly swallows up another 30 minutes, and then it's time to pick up our friend from rehab from the station. He joins us around the kitchen table. Soon, two other people arrive unexpectedly, and we spend the afternoon sharing as the Holy Spirit leads us. I still have a desire to eat those delicious shortbread slices that I put out as a treat for our guests!

Evening

A friend treats the family to a chicken meal at Kentucky Fried Chicken that, blissfully, was much easier for me to cope with than last week's trip to McDonald's. I wasn't so hungry tonight, so it was easy to watch the family eat. After our meal, we went bowling. Once back home, we watched a movie until around 1:00 a.m.

DAY 27 – Saturday, November 23rd

Again, I woke up to the throb of Your love in my heart. I feel as though I didn't really sleep well last night. Stephen heads off quite quickly for his Alpha Course's Holy Spirit day. The kids are good this morning—they are busy with Monopoly, Play Dough, cookies and milk. Lunchtime arrives, and the babysitter arrives, which frees me up to go to the hairdresser.

Blonde Ambition

I prayed on the way to the hairdresser, because I was feeling a little bit nervous. I wanted to change the style or color of my hair. My reason for being nervous was because I have been going to the same hairdresser for years. Today, I went to a different salon with another stylist in the hopes of a slightly new look. The old blonde hair was a bit brassy, and I wanted something a bit more chic!

I had a great time at the salon, and had an opportunity to speak with the junior stylist. Last time, I saw her (the same junior stylist, but at a different salon) she shared that she couldn't drink water. Immediately, the Lord revealed through a word of knowledge that, as a child, she choked on a glass of water and developed a traumatic phobia. I offered to pray with her then, but she was a little bit shy.

The first words the young girl said were, "Will you still pray for me about the water?" I was utterly amazed! We spent the entire afternoon talking. She asked lots of questions, and I was able to share about Your love and my own healing testimony. Despite her initial request, she still didn't want me to pray for her. But she did take my telephone number, and I told her that I'd be delighted to meet and pray with her, if ever she changed her mind!

Thank You for answering my prayer about my hair, Lord. The highlights and lowlights are complimentary, and I really like the new look. As I type in this previous sentence, it is a poignant reminder of the highs and lows of this fast!

It's Not a Formula

As I walk home, I think how ridiculous it is that I should believe that doing a 40-day fast will release miracles. It's not a formula—it's all about being obedient, and the blessing that follows obedience. If you choose to entrust the anointing for miracles to me, then that is Your sovereign right, Lord. It is all right for me to pursue Your utmost, but silly to think that I can influence Your sovereign plan for my life. Yet, I long for the fullness of the ministry of Jesus.

When I came home, our babysitter gave me a lovely bouquet of pink roses. She is so precious. We had an hour together and then she had to go to work. Stephen came home, but his day was disappointing. What a shame; I felt sad for him. People were not really interested in getting prayer for more of the Holy Spirit. Everyone who attended was a Christian, but I can't believe that no one wanted more of You, dear One!

I am sick of not eating and have reverted to being "Mrs. Moaning." Oh dear, I want to eat. I don't feel especially hungry, but I do crave a bit of variety. Thirteen days to go, but the end seems so far away. I intend to lie on the sofa tonight and be very lazy. Douglas has been invited to speak at tomorrow night's evening service at church—that's excellent!

Evening – TV and Some Healing

On television, I watch *An Audience with Donny Osmond*. It's like taking a trip down memory lane, and I am astounded at how emotional I feel. (When I was a teenager, I was an avid fan of Donny's music.). Tonight, when he sang "Twelfth of Never," something stirred deep within me. The melody resonates in my heart, "Until the twelfth of never and that's a long, long time..." Those lyrics remind me of how much You love us, Lord. Your Love is eternal.

Stephen and I watch a videotape of a light-hearted, romantic drama. The final scene portrays two young teenage girls about to head off to fulfill their future ambitions, hopes and dreams. I am oddly affected by the ending; I think to myself, "It wasn't like that for me." I feel small and teenaged again, and the film's ending—coupled with the Donny Osmond moment—triggers an unexpected, tear-filled response.

I go to bed, lie down and deluge myself in sobbing. Stephen comes in and holds me. I ask You, "Why I am crying?" Your tender voice breaks into my sorrowful heart, and You say, *"Child these are the tears that terror has held silent captives for many years. It is time to release them to me."* In the midst of it all, I am keenly aware that obedience is better than sacrifice. This thought resounds strongly in my spirit.

I lie in my bed crying tears held in the deepest recesses of my soul—until now. The pain is searing, and I fall asleep with my pillow wet with tears. Sobbing, I know Your arms are around me, as You let me cry the tears that no child should ever have to weep.

DAY 28 - Sunday, November 24th

I awaken to puffy eyelids and a bursting, sore head. Stephen and our youngest son, Samuel, both have head colds, so they stay home from church. Driving to church, I meditate on the tears that I wept last night. I attribute them to the fast and to reaching a new place of trusting You, my heavenly Father. I think of the ballad "The Twelfth of Never" and want to cry again. You speak to me, *"Precious child it was necessary to release those tears. I have held them for this time that I might heal you."* I am once again struck that submission to Your will is of great worth in Your sight. I want to be obedient, Lord.

Church is beautiful. The Pastor preaches on obedience—it's a timely message for me. At the end of the service, a young man gives me a personal prophetic word straight from Your heart. The word is surprisingly accurate. I wasn't looking for a blessing, Lord, but You confirm such beautiful things that You have spoken to me. You speak of grace, and the diamond that You gave me a few years ago in a vision. The prophet describes the scene just as it occurred: he sees You hand me a diamond and then the diamond becomes a rose. I am undone by the roses and the lavishness of Your care.

You are showering me with Your amazing love and outrageous grace. You speak to me through another believer: he describes the mountain of faith I have climbed, the pain of the journey, and the devotion of my heart for You. He speaks of my weariness and desire to be fully united with You. He is describing the path of humility and sacrifice, which leads to indescribable blessing through intimacy with You. I am experiencing these things in a new way through this fast. You speak of my call to the lost, the poor, the children, and to changing governments, and to bringing many to salvation.

Oh, Lord, You spoke so many wonderful things to me, and confirmed so many promises. I am overwhelmed. Yet, as I think on these promises Lord, I realize that they are not for me alone, but are part of the Great Commission given to the Church (see Matthew 28:18-20). These promises are for Your bride. (We arrive back home and share Sunday lunch. Ha ha, I wish I could! We have some time for our friend from rehab to leave, and then we clear up.)

Evening

After teatime, I head off to pick up my editor so we can attend the evening service. Worship is difficult this evening. We sing of being rescued, but a sense of unbelief rests upon God's people tonight. I read from Colossians about the supremacy of Christ, and affirm that He has rescued us from the dominion of darkness.

My friend shares a powerful word on living in the reality of the freedom that Christ purchased for us by His blood. Some of the young worshippers get their feet washed, while others come forward for ministry. I am delighted to be able to help with the deliverance ministry. One lovely lady gets released from demonic bondages. Your Kingdom comes with love and power, Lord. We return home at around 11:00 p.m., tired but deeply encouraged.

CHAPTER 8

Week Five: Meltdown at McDonald's

DAY 29 – Monday, November 25th

*M*y editor arrives in the morning, and we spend the entire day talking and sharing. I feel so vulnerable. I am frustrated in talking about my past, because I am not that person any more. By the end of the day, I am worn out and exhausted. Yet, I know that this process is necessary to unearth nuggets of gold for the manuscript, which is about my life and testimony.

DAY 30 – Tuesday, November 26th

I prayed with Stephen about the intense discouragement I felt upon waking up. The task of rewriting the book overwhelms me—it seems impossible. But I know, in the depth of my being, that all things are possible with You, Lord. Revisiting my past with my editor is such a strange, but necessary place to be. I don't like it very much: the person I am describing is not who I am, but who I was.

My first appointment today is with the team for our ladies' outreach. We meet early to plan and pray for "Change." We are shocked that the time has come around so quickly. There's only one week to go!

Ed arrives mid-morning and we begin work on the book again. I share my heart, and he sums it up in a lovely phrase, "It is the woe and the wonder of it all." The woe part made me feel discouraged, but the wonder of God in all of it encourages me! We agree on the way forward.

Afternoon – Stretched But Not Snapping

Everyone calls today—the phone just rings constantly. I forgot that a friend from America was touring Scotland and she arrived today. She calls hoping to meet me; I am in dilemma. Should I travel to Glasgow tonight to meet her? I don't feel that I want to travel on my own; I am already committed to attending the youth group to hand out fliers for "Change" to the mothers who are picking up their children. I decide to call her after 6 p.m., and then wait for the Lord's direction.

Another dear comrade calls three times from Denver, and I return his call. Yet, we still manage to miss each other! I am still trying to set up our meeting in Dublin on December 8th. Then another friend arrives, just after I pick up the kids from school. We spend time together, and I feel really encouraged. She has been faithfully praying for the outreach. Thank You, Jesus, for my dear young friend.

Evening

After dinner, the telephone continues to ring incessantly. Rebecca wants me to help her with making party invitations. Daniel wants me to help with his homework. I need to print off 40 fliers, and my head hurts with all this multi-tasking! Amidst all this, I managed to call my American friend "on tour," and we spend a lovely 30 minutes chatting and praying.

I do get everything done. Stephen looks after the kids, while I pick up Daniel from church group, help with the youth and hand out fliers. I come home, help with the dispatch and flop down. My head feels like a mass of jelly.

DAY 31 – Wednesday, November 27th

My editor is sick: the poor soul is down-and-out with the flu! I finally manage to connect with my friend from Denver. We have agreed that I will fly out on the 8th and meet them in London. My fasting buddy comes by and we have a good old chat—no prayers or anything else spiritual, we just spend time hanging out. I intend to update my diary, and then not do too much thinking or talking today.

I love You, Lord. In mid-morning, I realize that I have no book. I am utterly distraught. I feel as if I have wasted an entire year and a half writing a book that no longer exists, because we have edited so much of it away. I started the writing process only with prophetic revelation, and now that's basically all I have left. I hate this book. I weep and weep. I am sick of trying to write this book and hear from God. I am even angry with You, Lord.

Afternoon

I spend most of the afternoon crying. I go to school to pick up Samuel. A believer encourages me to press in for the breakthrough. I know she's right, but I am struggling to press through the pain barrier and on into victory.

Evening

Two of my spiritual sons come by this evening. We spend a long time talking about the book as well as our relationships in the Kingdom. I ask lots of questions. All I hear God say is, "Write the book for Jacob." These guys are my friends, and they are the Jacob generation. I feel restored. I still loathe the book, but just not as much.

DAY 32 - Thursday, November 28th

I don't dislike the book so much today, but I still feel wiped out. Vulnerability and transparency are choices in grace. I go for a swim. My editor is much better today. We talk some more. I tell him that I hate the book. He smiles and says, "Good, that's just when an author needs an editor." I cry some more.

Afternoon – Visiting the Psychic Lady

My friend and I pay a visit to the psychic lady I met before. Her husband swears a lot, and she is a racist. Oh my! We smile when she mentions that she told her tarot card friends that two young Christian women are holding an alternative predictions night! What a paradox that she sees prophecy as an alternative!

I share some more with my editor, and then I weep some more with him too! The book is forming. Deep down in my spirit, I feel it coming together, despite the fact we still haven't lifted the manuscript! In the midst of this process, I realize that I don't have to apologize for the fact that the establishment almost crushed me. I can tell that part of my story: it isn't about rebellion—it's about an invasion of righteousness.

DAY 33 – Friday, November 29th 5 p.m.

Meltdown at McDonald's

We went to McDonald's. I sat down at the cold Formica table, glared out the glass window into the dark night, and, in a split-second of hunger-induced-madness, I made the decision to eat. I asked Stephen to order me a Big Mac. He looked at me curiously and said, "Are you sure?" My silence and sullen stare were formidable answers, and he proceeded to buy me the requested meal. I sat alone at the table as my bewildered family tried not to stare. I ate like a pig, and shoved huge pieces of cheeseburger and fries into my mouth at an alarming rate. I was so angry with myself for eating, but, at the same time, I couldn't stop now that I had started.

We travelled home in silence. I sat, quiet and stunned, in my kitchen. I couldn't believe what I had just done. My fast was over. I felt as though I had been riding a bicycle at full speed and had unexpectedly fallen off. I was shocked and felt numb.

DAY 34 – Saturday, November 30th

Upon waking, I wonder if I could start my fast again. I am thinking that I might be able to get back on my bike, so to speak. I really hadn't meant to eat last night—it just sort of "happened." I was frustrated at my lack of self-control. I've decided to try again. God said 40 days, so I'm going to try for 40 days. I am an idiot!

I am ravenous! I've changed my mind. By 4 p.m. my resolve to fast has dissolved completely. I eat the Chinese meal sitting on our table, and reconcile myself to the fact I have completed a 33-day fast.

DAY 35 – Sunday, December 1st

We attended our local Church of Scotland this morning and had a beautiful service. Samuel stood up and began to clap as soon as the worship began, and that was so encouraging! Because it was St Andrew's Day, a young man played bagpipes at the end of service. A strange phenomenon took place during this time: both Stephen and I were reduced to floods of tears. In my heart, I was thinking of how much I personally love Scotland and how much the Lord adores our nation. I was reminded that bagpipes have a place in heavenly worship, and my soul burst open with love for this people and this land.

Alongside this, a distinct voice gently requested that I get ready to leave. I do not know if the departing is temporary or permanent, but I do know that my poor heart was turned inside-out by the very thought of it. The pain of leaving was already almost unbearable. Still, I understood that the call is costly, but Jesus is worth it.

Afternoon – Car Crash

In the afternoon, I decide to visit my stepfather and his fiancée. After a lovely cup of tea and chat, I left their house only to carelessly back our car into the front of another vehicle. I was completely disgusted with myself for being so careless. We've only had our car for a couple of months, and the damage seems quite extensive. The other car I reversed into was old and beat-up and, literally, didn't have a scratch. By contrast, I could hardly believe what a mess ours was. After insurance, the added costs will be £200, and the initial damage looks to cost somewhere in range of £500 to £600. What a dreadful time of year for this to happen, and it's so close to the ladies' outreach meeting!

DAY 36 – Monday, December 2nd

We have another team meeting for "Change." I'm disappointed that only 30 women are coming along, and six of them are non-Christians. We talk, and pray through the situation. We are going to take up an offering during the ladies meeting, and the proceeds will be donated to the women's prison at Stirling. The thought of returning to the women's prison invigorates me, and, perhaps, the door will remain open for an opportunity to minister the gospel.

Evening – The Drunken Damsel in Distress

Tonight, I helped a lady in the street who was being harassed by some youths. I was on my way home with a friend when we saw her. We brought the woman into the car, and shared Jesus' love with her. I've seen this same lady on the street several times, but I haven't been able to speak with her for two reasons: one is that she has always been helplessly drunk; and two, on those occasions I have had one or more of the children with me. Tonight was different: the children were at home, so my friend and I could spend some quality time with this woman.

My heart went out to her, but my nose recoiled at the smell of this dear one. Her clothes were stained and unwashed, she had matted hair, and the stench of urine was almost unbearable. Help me to overcome my sensitivities, Lord. She managed to scribble down her address on a piece of paper for me. I am now more than convinced that if I start a lunch club, then people like this lady will come and we can begin to establish relationships with them. The daunting task of reaching the poorest of society overwhelms me, but I long to do it for love of Christ. I think of the Gadarene man in the Bible, a deranged individual whose life was completely transformed through Christ's love; I remind myself that no one is beyond the saving grace of Jesus. My own life is a testimony to this truth!

DAY 37 – Tuesday, December 3rd

I am fully convinced that Jesus is my friend, and I am a friend to Him. It's been a process of personal discovery on this journey of intimacy, but I notice that even my language uses the term "Jesus" as one would towards a friend. Previously, I would say Lord, Father, Master, or Teacher, but rarely the name "Jesus" as one would speak to a friend. That Jesus desires friendship with His children is an awesome privilege and a deep yet simple truth

My editor is busy this afternoon, so I try to visit my sister and then a friend, but no one is home! My poor little niece has chicken pox, so we haven't seen each other in a while. I have a message to prepare for tomorrow night, which I will do later. Stephen is taking his buddy to the movies and then out eat for a 40th birthday celebration.

DAY 38 – Wednesday, December 4th

Learning to Weather the Storm

I go for a drive, and park the car at the beach. The sky is grey, and the wind is howling all around me. My car gets buffeted by the strong gales. I watch the sea, as its waves crash wildly on the rocks—it is a stark picture of winter wonder. The waves and the rocks weather the storm together.

My eyes rise towards Heaven. A lone seagull being lifted up and down in the wind catches my attention. The bird is not flapping, and not even struggling—it is simply gliding on the wind's undercurrent beneath its wings. I marvel at the bird's surrender to the mighty wind that envelops it. The bird goes with the current's flow and is carried along effortlessly. Time stands still as I ponder the surrender of my own heart to You, Lord. I am blessed watching this storm ravaged picture of cooperative creation, which is beautiful in all its rugged splendor.

DAY 39 – Thursday, December 5th

I have nothing to say. I'm still thinking about the solitary seagull and its resolute courage in surrender. I want to be that yielded to Christ. At times, I still struggle to take control when the best decision I could make is simply to yield, be enveloped in God's mighty presence and wrap myself in a garland of His grace.

DAY 40 – Friday, December 6th

Today, I should be celebrating the end of my 40-day fast. Instead, in somewhat resigned fashion, I think about the fact that I stopped a week before I had intended. This is Rebecca's 7th birthday. The children arrived for the party, but Rebecca decided not to dress up or have her face painted. Maybe she felt a little miserable just like I did? Looking at the table that I decorated with roses and some beautiful princess paper, I felt slightly annoyed that Rebecca didn't want to be the center of attention. Today was her special day. She was grumpy, and I felt slightly irritated about that. For different reasons, we both felt a tinge of disappointment.

Soon after, Rebecca and I had a good cry, and then we reconciled to each other again. Rebecca decided that she would get her face painted. In the midst of all this, a little girl got annoyed that she couldn't wear a particular princess outfit, since another guest already asked to wear it. We didn't realize it, but that upset little girl left the house. Five minutes later, we discovered our guest list was one child short. Thankfully, the girl, who lived next door, had not gone too far. Nonetheless, we had a terrible panic while searching for a missing five year old! I couldn't believe I nearly lost a birthday guest!

Despite a somewhat shaky start, the party ended really well. The adults ended up getting dressed up as well. My fasting buddy was with me, and we truly enjoyed having fun with our children and also being childlike ourselves. I was reminded of how much my fasting journey involved learning to be like a child, and depend on God for my needs.

Deep down inside, we felt like princesses and laughed outrageously as we adorned ourselves in fluffy, pink feather boas and sparkling tiaras. We celebrated Rebecca's birthday meal in extravagance, with a vase of pink roses as a centerpiece to a lovely, pale pink tablecloth. The girls dined on princess plates, topped with the finest strawberries and other special treats. We have a Kodak picture to remind us of the moment, which imprinted God's goodness to us on our hearts.

CHAPTER 9

What Did I Learn?

$\mathcal{M}$arvelling at the Lord's love seems an appropriate way to end those extraordinary 40 days with Jesus. We can do nothing to earn or merit the Lord's love. Knowing that Jesus delights in us is a place of absolute affirmation and acceptance. There is no stronger foundation on which we can build our lives: that of the love of God, our heavenly Father, cast wide in our hearts by the Holy Spirit. Jesus longs for intimacy with each one of His precious children.

I have come to realize that fasting is a way to touch the deepest recesses of His heart. Fasting is a means of turning away from everything that distracts us from a full embrace of the Father's arms.

This fast was a journey into the depths of Jesus' love. When I began the fast, I had no idea what an emotional roller coaster the next six weeks would prove to be. I lost almost every comfort zone I had; I plummeted into the depths of self-despair, and ascended the heights of ecstatic worship. My emotions seesawed from grumpy, irritable, weepy, and tired to being full of peace, joy and love. But my momentary discomfort soon gave way to spiritual joys.

ENDURANCE – GETHSEMANE'S GIFT

At the beginning of my 40-day experience, I had a sense that the Lord wanted to teach me about endurance. Truthfully, I had only a vague notion of what that might mean. Now some two years later, as I complete *Confessions of a Fasting Housewife*, I have a clearer picture in my heart of what it means to receive the gift of endurance. My perception of what God did during my fast has broadened and blossomed with time. The broad strokes of my understanding now have fine-tuned details of revelation brushed-in as highlights on the pages of my life.

Throughout the ups and downs of my fast, Jesus taught me much, not least of all which was the need to stick to the task set before me. Endurance means having stamina in the face of adversity, showing fortitude amidst difficult circumstances, and displaying staying power even when everything within us wants to run and hide! Endurance teaches us patience and humility. Above all endurance is a gift of grace from the Lord, and it enables us to be obedient to our heavenly Father.

When I reflect of Jesus in the Garden of Gethsemane, I see the incredible beauty and costliness of His suffering. Endurance was Jesus' gift from the Father that enabled Him to be obedient unto death, even death on the Cross. Obedience to the Father's will in our life releases Gethsemane's gift—endurance—which, in turn, enables us not to deny God. Endurance is a precursor to the glory of God being released in our lives. What a precious jewel of revelation to receive!

LEARNING TO EMBRACE THE CROSS

Other jewels of revelation marked the milestones of my 40-day pilgrimage with Christ. Learning to embrace the Cross was such a foundational aspect of the journey. As I studied the Cross, I came to cherish our Lord's sacrifice, suffering and glory in a measure I had never known before. The Cross is the place of transformation, where the ashes of our self-life are resurrected into Kingdom beauty.

During the fast, the Lord showed me that nothing can be taken to the Cross, except for our heavenly Father's blessing and approval. This hidden and solitary place is where the Holy Spirit effects deep and lasting change. The Cross is the place where we are emptied out, and where our hearts experience divine agitation towards a greater place of servant love and healing. Here, we discover that we are truly cherished, as the Holy Spirit tenderly crucifies in us the language of "I".

WHAT CHANGED?

At times, weariness almost overtook me, and I felt like giving up on more than one occasion. Through my tiredness, tears, numbness, depression and discouragement, the beauty of the Cross continued to pound my heart with exquisite precision; it fashioned me to be something for God's glory, and taught me that even when all I have to offer is my tears, they are enough. On some occasions, the defining lines between Heaven and earth seemed blurred. But the passage of time has helped me define and re-focus what God has done, and is still doing, through that fast.

This fast brought about many changes in me as a person, with some being more obvious than others. For instance, the huge weight loss was easily discernible. However, numerous other changes also took place inside of me, which were far less noticeable.

CHOICES & CONSEQUENCES

Fasting taught me about the impact that choices have on my day-to-day life. When our choices in life become Christ-centred, these God-encounter moments help us relinquish what we consider to be our rights. I learned to give up my right to have a reputation, to have ambitions, and, indeed, to have any rights at all! I surrendered my right to self-pity and to sulking, but sadly not without a fight! Accessing the pathway called "denial of self" is only possible in God's grace.

I found that as I was sifted like flour, over and over again, each time a further impurity was removed from my heart. Jealousy, pride, insecurity, and materialism were exposed one by one. God's perfect love examined the motivation of my heart, until my Kingdom identity began to shine through more clearly.

The Lord has taught me to pace myself, to be resilient and to be devoted to Him—no matter how weak I might feel. As we surrender to His ways, His grace sweeps upon us and lifts us into victory. Ultimately, God's grace enabled me to persevere and break through into various levels of personal victory: these included surrendering to God's will in my life, being patient with myself, and trusting Jesus more than I ever had previously.

LEARNING TO LIVE A PRAYER OF LOVE

Throughout the fast, I learned to love more deeply than I ever thought possible. Some moments, I thought my heart would break wide open with the pain of not being perfectly united with Jesus in glory. The agonies of longing for Him etched deep scars of love into my soul. Like a woman's stretch marks after giving birth, these scars of great beauty speak of a life hidden in Christ.

In moments of extreme hunger I sometimes felt greedier than a person ever ought to. Yet, there were moments when—in my desperate desire for food—my inner man fed fully on Christ's manifest presence. Jesus sustained me. With his perspective, I saw in a more exaggerated way than ever before. I was more sensitive in noticing hurting people all around me. Drunkards, drug addicts, lonely and broken-hearted people became my concern. As I thought of their pain and isolation, the anointing for intercession ran like oil down upon my head. I prayed until my exhausted lips could speak no more words.

Conversely, I could barely whisper a prayer on other occasions. At such times, I began to understand that my silent or liquid-tear prayers were perfectly valid, Kingdom expressions. Ultimately, the travail served to bring me into a greater revelation of Jesus' joy.

TOKENS OF DIVINE AFFECTION

Throughout this fast, I was astonished by the tokens of divine affection that I received. The dreams, visions, revelations and unexpected gifts—such as the bouquets of roses and the perfect china cup-and-saucer—all spoke deeply of God's tender loving care in my life. My husband was a great support most of the time, except for very occasional moments when we became verbal sparring partners. Stephen's love reinforced Jesus' role as both my Maker and my Husband. Waves of worship would sometimes break over me, and I would lose myself in wonder of our magnificent Saviour. In some small way, I have learned to dream the way God thinks. I have a crown of salvation, and it is my great joy to cast it down in adoration at the feet of Christ!

Every day, I sought the sweet and perfect presence of Jesus. Without actual fresh bread in my diet, I became keenly aware of my spiritual hunger; the need to seek fresh manna of Jesus' presence consumed my waking moments. Sometimes, the Lord would answer my heart's desire to be with Him and I would sense His presence immediately. At other times, the silence taught me to listen carefully for His voice and to discern truth from the counterfeit. I pursued and persisted until able to clearly discern God's voice and that of the accuser. At such a vulnerable time in my life, being able to distinguish between the two opposing voices was important.

SOLITUDE – A CRUCIBLE TO CHERISH

During this fast, solitude was the crucible that Christ used to refine my relationship with Him. In silence, my Savior's love fastened me close to His heartbeat, and anchored me in a strong, sure foundation of faith. My longing for Jesus reflects the Father's longing for His children, and Jesus' longing for His bride—it speaks of a coming age, when we will be perfectly united with Christ in glory. Divine union is the greatest of all graces granted to the Church: it is the most exquisite yet heartrending experience, but I would not swap it for all the riches in Heaven or earth.

Amid some intense personal challenges, I believe that the fast produced fruit that will last for all eternity. Through ill health, bed-wetting, potty training, broken vases, scribbled walls, car crashes and phone lines breaking down, God reigned supreme! In the midst of all this chaos, God wanted to teach me to receive His peace—even in conflict. In the thick of laundry, shopping, cleaning the toilet and writing sermons, Jesus mentored and nurtured me as His disciple. In the pruning, God pared back my "soulish" hiding places—such as the occasional chocolate binge or shopping spree—and taught me to take refuge in Him alone. As the fast progressed, the things of this world ceased to distract me in the degree that they had previously.

Aspects of Christ's lovely nature became more evident with each passing week of the fast. He is King, Father, Friend, Bridegroom and so much more. The very nature of Christ was revealed in the beautiful way He transformed my odd moments of self-loathing and perceived failure into mini-miracles of His compassion and mercy. Again and again, the Holy Spirit reinforced various aspects of salvation— acceptance, forgiveness and unconditional love, to name but a few. The Father's song was a lullaby in my soul, and it sealed the healing He outworked in my heart. I discovered that Jesus sees the potential for Kingdom beauty in everything.

CHAPTER 10

Blossom!

*I*n early April 2003, spring was beginning to break out in our village. My little cherry tree had been barren through the winter, but was now starting to bud and blossom. Just like me! Cherry blossom is my absolute favorite tree. When wind blows pink blossoms off the branches, I am always reminded of confetti adorning the pavement after a couple is married. Likewise, cherry blossoms strewn in the street make me think of the second coming of Jesus Christ, when He returns to the earth to unite with His beautiful Bride—the Church—for all eternity.

Just before I left for New England to launch my first book, a dear friend gave me a beautiful teddy bear named "Blossom." My friend was unaware of my love for cherry blossoms, and I was touched by her kind gesture. I would later discover that this gift had great significance. So in mid-April, I left home to meet up with my editor. Upon arriving in Boston, I began narrating the cherry tree story to him. At the exact moment of my telling him about the blossom, we passed by a solitary white cherry tree in full bloom. We were staggered by its beauty, and by the God-inspired coincidence of finding such a tree at that exact moment. It was a mini-miracle of nature!

We saw no further cherry trees until we arrived in Connecticut. As we drove along, we remarked at the extraordinary number of cherry trees there. However, none of them had yet to bloom. When we arrived at the church, a soft and extraordinary warm spring wind was blowing. By the time we left Connecticut, on the next day, and drove to Vermont, the trees had literally bloomed overnight. I awoke to a breathtaking display of pale pink cherry blossom. My heart was moved deeply, and I received this as a gift from God. Despite the winter I had known during my long fast, spring had finally arrived and a season of fruitfulness and glory came with it. Just as nature celebrates the end of winter by heralding bright yellow daffodil trumpets, so my heart was soaring at these new beginnings. Blossom, the teddy bear, had been a prophetic gift indeed!

Christian maturity is an ongoing process that involves many cycles and seasons with the Lord, so as to bring about Godly transformation. God's "suddenly" is usually preceded by a "winter" season, when a person is pruned in preparation for new growth being brought about by the Holy Spirit. Spiritual winters enable us to be strengthened for Kingdom fruitfulness. In other words, we are pruned in preparation to blossom! This fast was much like a winter season: it was one of the most difficult yet blessed spiritual experiences I have ever known, and was only made possible through God's love and kindness. Yet, I did not remain in my "winter" season forever, for the Lord gloriously enabled me to blossom for Him in a fresh season of springtime joy and wonder!

Jesus invited me to walk with Him on this journey. What a journey of God-discovery and self-discovery it proved to be! I relearned the value of writing a journal, and that has been most worthwhile, as it prompted my memories and the text for this book. I began *Confessions of A Fasting Housewife* by inviting you, the reader, to join me on my 40-day, maiden fasting voyage. Now that the book is almost over, one more thing remains: Jesus extends a royal invitation to each one of YOU to personally to fast for His glory.

A FAMILY OF GLOBAL FASTERS

All over the world, there are people who love Jesus with everything, and who simply want to honor Him with their lives. I believe myself to be part of a global family of believers, who are pursuing the Kingdom with every bit of strength. God is asking us to fast together for His glory. What a radical thought: in these end times, the Lord would grant His grace to a global army of believers to defeat the kingdom of darkness through fasting, prayer, worship and sacrificial love!

It is my heart's desire that in sharing some of my journey, you will be inspired to press in for all that Jesus has for you and your Kingdom destiny. If you are in a winter season, take heart: spring will surely come, and you will produce wonderful fruit for eternity. May you blossom for His glory!

I suppose that the million-dollar question is "Would I do it all over again?" Despite being stretched and, at times, stricken, the answer is: yes, I do intend on doing it all over again. Perhaps a more pointed question at this juncture is: Will you? The invitation is before you. Beloved, what will you choose? Did I get my miracle anointing? Well, we'll just have to wait and see...?

EPILOGUE

What Happened Next?

*I*f you are like me, and don't enjoy loose ends, then perhaps you will benefit from this summary of some temporal aspects of my 40 days with Jesus.

I don't know what my final weight was by the end of the fast. I gave up weighing myself when I got down to one specific pair of trousers that fit me. After returning to my usual food intake, my weight averaged out at around 133 pounds, which is almost 14 pounds lighter than when I began the fast.

My teeth and tongue returned to normal, and the shrinking gums feelings receded with my final hunger pangs. My manners at meal times have definitely improved: I have not once dipped my finger in a gravy boat, or drank leftover liquid from a can of peas! My Kleenex tissue supply is now greatly reduced, and my emotions returned to "normal" along with my weight.

My hair has been several different shades of blonde now and—apart from one do-it-yourself disaster on the hair front—the highlights and lowlights continued to remind me of my life-changing, 33-day, blonde ambition fast!

I continue to hate cancer with a passion, and I am delighted to say that the pastor and the prophet who were suffering from cancer both got healed!

Blissfully, Samuel became fully potty trained! One evening, he tore diaper and said, "I don't want to wear this anymore," and has been dry at night ever since, with only one or two minor transgressions in the bed-wetting arena.

My fasting buddy successfully completed her 40-day fast. My spiritual daughter decided to go to university and is currently in her first year of classes. My spiritual sons continue to press in for all that God has prepared for them. I did finally meet with my comrade from Denver—it was a blessed time in the airport lounge of a London airport, and well worth the effort.

Rebecca and Daniel each had a tonsillectomy in September 2003. The two siblings were in and out of hospital in a matter of days, and each of them made a full recovery with no lasting ill effects. Remarkably, Mark is beginning to develop a liking for my cooking. Although if steak pie is on the menu, we still have a hunger striker on our hands. Our trips to the orthodontist are fairly peaceful these days, and Mark is persevering well with his braces. We continue to enjoy family trips to McDonald's, and I no longer find it a traumatic place to be on Friday evenings.

Our friend successfully completed his drug rehabilitation program at Teen Challenge, has since graduated, and is now pursuing life-on-the-outside in the northeast of Scotland

Stephen's business has continued to flourish, although we have not yet seen the explosion that I saw in my vision. However, we are believing for an increase.

The car was repaired, and although it cost us more than £200, we were relieved that it didn't cost a huge amount to fix. The car was a gift from the Lord, and He has continued to grace us with His provision for fuel and car maintenance.

In December 2002, we finally had our ladies' outreach meeting, "Change." Around 50 women, turned up for dinner, drama, crafts and an evening of fellowship. We had a gift table from which ladies could help themselves to anything they would like—either for themselves or a friend. At the meeting, we collected money to later donate to Corton Vale Women's prison in Stirling. Shortly after, we visited the prison and gave the gift to Sister Monica, one of the prison chaplains, in person. The cash gift was used to purchase a CD player for Christian services in the prison.

My editor returned to the States and my first book, *The Normal, the Deep and the Crazy*, was completed in a whirlwind of activity. It was launched in New England in April 2003.

APPENDIX I

More About Fasting

*T*his is not intended to be an exhaustive study of fasting. If it includes any glaring omissions, all I can say is "I'm sorry and be patient—I'm learning too!" I've put together a Biblical foundation for fasting, and have restricted the text to themes with a supporting Scripture passage. May you be mightily blessed as you explore this vast subject with Jesus. It's all about Him!

GOD'S WORD SHOWS US WE SHOULD FAST

If the Bible is any indication, the Word reveals that fasting releases us to be overcomers:

"Even now," declares the Lord, "return to me with all your heart, with fasting and weeping and mourning" (Joel 2:12).

Rather, as servants of God we commend ourselves in every way: in great endurance; in troubles, hardships and distresses; in beatings, imprisonments and riots; in hard work, sleepless nights and hunger; in purity, understanding, patience and kindness; in the Holy Spirit and in sincere love; (2 Corinthians 6:4-6).

FRIENDS OF THE BRIDEGROOM (JESUS) WANT TO FAST

Fasting is one expression of bridal intimacy with Christ.

Jesus answered, "How can the guests of the bridegroom mourn while he is with them? The time will come when the bridegroom will be taken from them; then they will fast" (Matthew 9:15).

WE FAST TO BECOME HUMBLE BEFORE GOD

Fasting helps move us from a place of self-reliance to God-reliance, and from independence to God-dependence. Fasting keeps you honest. The apostle James made this point abundantly clear: if you want power and grace from God, then you have to humble yourself. *"Humble yourselves before the Lord, and he will lift you up."* (James 4:10)

Fasting is a choice *for God* and *against the flesh*. When you fast, you make a conscious inward choice, which is demonstrated by an outward act, that you want God's power (and not your own power) to flow through you. You want God's answer, and not your own.

My knees give way from fasting; my body is thin and gaunt. I am an object of scorn to my accusers; when they see me, they shake their heads. Help me, O Lord my God; save me in accordance with your love. Let them know that it is your hand, that you, O Lord, have done it. They may curse, but you will bless… (Psalm 109:24-28).

FASTING TO OBTAIN HIS GRACE AND POWER

We fast to obtain God's grace and power. The Holy Spirit is called "the Spirit of Grace"—He enables us to become weak before God, so that God's power can flow through us. As we come to the end of ourselves, God can move through us in power. Humility is about weakness, or surrender, before God. As we yield to the Father, we become meek and—in our submission to His perfect will—God can use us to advance the Kingdom! And He said to me:

My grace is sufficient for you, for my power is made perfect in weakness." Therefore I will boast all the more gladly about my weaknesses, so that Christ's power may rest on me (2 Corinthians 12:9).

FASTING FOR PURITY

As the great pioneer of our faith, Jesus gives us a pattern for fasting. Jesus fasted for 40 days and nights, and came out of a wilderness of temptation in the power of the Spirit. Extended fasting (such as 40 days) is like an atomic bomb of God's power—it's part of His divine strategy for the Church to overcome the kingdom of darkness. If a habit or chronic sin keeps cropping up in your life, then humble your soul in fasting, and God will purify you.

Fasting for purity can be fairly confusing. The more you push in for purity, the more you seem to be conscious of impurity in your life! As you surrender to God, the Holy Spirit brings to the surface all the hidden sin in your life. You will soon notice—especially on longer fasts—that a hidden, bad temper will be exposed and you will start yelling at people. Other aspects like laziness, apathy, pride, greed, gluttony, grumbling, selfishness, jealousy and many more may surface as well. Let God heal you, and deal with that sin! Be patient and be encouraged, and don't give up.

FASTING FOR SALVATIONS, HEALINGS, DELIVERANCES AND MIRACLES

Having fasted for 40 days, Jesus left the wilderness in *power*! He overcame the devil in the power of the Holy Spirit, and then entered into an EXTREME ministry of salvations, healings, deliverances and divine miracles!

Jesus returned to Galilee in the power of the Spirit, and news about him spread through the whole countryside. He taught in their synagogues, and everyone praised him (Luke 4:14).

FASTING FOR BREAKTHROUGH

Sometimes, breakthrough comes during a fast, but other times it may come later on. Demonic obstructions may delay the breakthrough, but cannot deny it! (see Daniel 9,10) Every time you pray under the anointing *something happens*. You can count on that. Don't get discouraged and don't give up! Keep praying until something happens—PUSH!

FASTING FOR DELIVERANCE

Fasting is sometimes needed for deliverance.

After Jesus had gone indoors, his disciples asked him privately, "Why couldn't we drive it (the demon) out?" He replied, "This kind can come out only by prayer" (Mark 9:28-29).

FASTING AS A PART OF EVERY DAY MINISTRY

As part of His daily life, Jesus constantly ministered to people. In His first year of ministry, as recorded by Mark, He was totally inundated by requests for prayer and healing. He ministered to crowds everywhere non-stop, so He often missed meals: such was His devotion and dedication to His Father's will. His compassion for the multitudes meant that both He and His disciples frequently missed meals; in other words, they fasted! Thousands fasted with Him as they waited and listened to Christ, their teacher and healer. *"Then Jesus entered a house, and again a crowd gathered, so that he and his disciples were not even able to eat"* (Mark 3:20).

FASTING FOR PROVISION

We may need to fast when we need God's miraculous intervention.

When Jesus landed and saw a large crowd, he had compassion on them, because they were like sheep without a shepherd. So he began teaching them many things. By this time it was late in the day... (Mark 6:34-35).

FASTING FOR OTHERS

Prepare for the time when Jesus asks you to intercede and fast for the sins of others. Jesus and the prophet Daniel are awesome role models in this regard. Jonathan fasted from food because of his broken heart at his father Saul's treatment of David. Perhaps this abstinence from food was a conscious choice to fast and pray for David's safe deliverance?

Jonathan got up from the table in fierce anger; on that second day of the month he did not eat, because he was grieved at his father's shameful treatment of David (1 Samuel 20:34).

FROM ILLNESS

David fasted for others while they were ill. We can do likewise, and believe for a breakthrough healing anointing. *"Yet when they were ill, I put on sackcloth and humbled myself with fasting"* (Psalm 35:13a).

FASTING TO BIRTH GOD'S PROMISE

Sometimes, we need to fast to bring forth God's promise. Hannah was desperate for a son, and prayed for years without her prayers being answered. God eventually answered her prayers with a double-portion: an apostolic, prophetic, interceding, passionate, worshipping, priestly son in the shape of Samuel! Hannah persevered, sometimes going without food, and sometimes being broken-hearted, yet never giving up on the seed of promise in her heart. If you are holding a promise in your heart, then ask God if you are to fast and pray to birth it from Heaven to earth.

And because the LORD had closed her womb, her rival kept provoking her in order to irritate her. This went on year after year. Whenever Hannah went up to the house of the LORD, her rival provoked her till she wept and would not eat (1 Samuel 1:6-7).

THE DANIEL MODEL – FASTING FOR A NATION

Daniel was a righteous man who "stood in the gap" for his nation and repented for the sin of Israel. God heard his prayers, and sent an angel on the first day that Daniel started praying. God is still looking for men and women with the heart of Daniel to fast and pray for their nations!

So I turned to the Lord God and pleaded with him in prayer and petition, in fasting, and in sackcloth and ashes. I prayed to the LORD my God and confessed: "O Lord, the great and awesome God, who keeps his covenant of love with all who love him and obey his commands, we have sinned and done wrong. We have been wicked and have rebelled; we have turned away from your commands and laws" (Daniel 9:3-5).

We can use this same prayer as a model for fasting and repentance today. We can pray it for our personal situations, our children, our parents, our friends, our congregations, our cities and our nations. The Scriptures say, "God, *we* have sinned. We have departed from *Your* ways, O God. We are in defeat because of *our* sins and transgressions. Please forgive *us*."

THE JONAH MODEL – FASTING FOR A CITY

At times, entire cities or nations may need to fast to repent and be purified from sin. This happened in Jonah's day. The Ninevites were a wicked, violent people who were about to be judged and annihilated by God, but then *they went on a fast* (even the donkeys, camels, and goats were put on a fast!):

The Ninevites believed God. They declared a fast, and all of them, from the greatest to the least, put on sackcloth. When the news reached the king of Nineveh, he rose from his throne, took off his royal robes, covered himself with sackcloth and sat down in the dust. Then he issued a proclamation in Nineveh: "By the decree of the king and his nobles: Do not let any man or beast, herd or flock, taste anything; do not let them eat or drink. But let man and beast be covered with sackcloth. Let everyone call urgently on God. Let them give up their evil ways and their violence. Who knows? God may yet relent and with compassion turn from his fierce anger so that we will not perish." When God saw what they did and how they turned from their evil ways, he had compassion and did not bring upon them the destruction he had threatened (Jonah 3:5-10).

FASTING IN TIMES OF CRISIS TO OBTAIN MERCY

In times of crisis, the Bible shows us how men and women have turned to God in prayer and fasting. Radical times call for radical solutions! Esther was a humble woman of God seeking His intervention in her nation's great crisis. Haman was set to wipe out the entire Jewish nation in one blow. During Esther's days, the Jews had not yet been dispersed to the four corners of the earth. The king of the Persians and Medes had already signed the death warrant when Esther commanded the Jews to observe a fast: then she risked her life to enter the king's presence to obtain mercy and pardon for her people.

Then Esther sent this reply to Mordecai: "Go, gather together all the Jews who are in Susa, and fast for me. Do not eat or drink for three days, night or day. I and my maids will fast as you do. When this is done, I will go to the king, even though it is against the law. And if I perish, I perish" (Esther 4:15-16).

Esther observed a three-day fast of total abstinence from food and water, and she asked the entire nation to do the same. The end result was that God turned the crisis around, and brought deliverance to the Jewish people to save the entire nation. Total abstinence from food and water is the most aggressive fast of all. Please seek medical advice before embarking on such a fast, and we recommend no more than three-day stints on this particular one!

FASTING WHEN YOU NEED GOD'S ANSWERS AND YOU DON'T HAVE ANY!

In 2 Chronicles 20, Judah was about to be destroyed by their enemies. King Jehoshaphat had no idea what to do, but he trusted God! He instructed the people to fast and pray. Then, he sent out a team of worshippers before his armies, and exalted the holiness of God. Ultimately, God delivered the people, and set an ambush against their enemies. If you feel surrounded by your enemy, then maybe you need to fast and worship!

Alarmed, Jehoshaphat resolved to inquire of the LORD, and he proclaimed a fast for all Judah. The people of Judah came together to seek help from the LORD (2 Chronicles 20:3-4).

After consulting the people, Jehoshaphat appointed men to sing to the LORD and to praise him for the splendour of his holiness as they went out at the head of the army... As they began to sing and praise, the LORD set ambushes against the men... (2 Chronicles 20:21-22).

FASTING FOR GOD'S DIRECTION

When you need God's direction, solution, or intervention, or are confused about what decision to make, one of the best things to do is to *fast*. If you are looking for L-O-V-E in the area of personal relationships and marriage, then fasting is also an excellent way of hearing God's heart, as it will help you to make the right choice about whom to marry.

There, by the Ahava Canal, I proclaimed a fast, so that we might humble ourselves before our God and ask him for a safe journey for us and our children, with all our possessions. I was ashamed to ask the king for soldiers and horsemen to protect us from ene-mies on the road, because we had told the king, "The gracious hand of our God is on everyone who looks to him, but his great anger is against all who forsake him." So we fasted and petitioned our God about this, and he answered our prayer (Ezra 8:21-23).

FASTING AS AN ACT OF WORSHIP

Anna was a New Testament prophetess who fasted DAILY because of her devotion to her King. Anna lived a fasted lifestyle, and that fasting flowed from her desire to worship God. What a role model she is! Her fasting released prophetic accuracy and truth, and brought her into deeper levels of revelation and divine understanding. The Bible does not record her specific words over the baby Jesus, but it is not unreasonable to believe that she prophesied with heavenly sig-nificance at the time of Christ's birth.

There was also a prophetess, Anna, the daughter of Phaneul, of the tribe of Asher. She was very old; she had lived with her husband seven years after her marriage, and then was a widow until she was eighty-four. She never left the temple but worshipped night and day, fasting and praying. Coming up to them that very moment, she gave thanks to God and spoke about the child to all who were looking forward to the redemption of Jerusalem (Luke 2:36-38).

FASTING FOR UNDERSTANDING AND
DIVINE REVELATION

As believers, we need more than direction. We need *revelation* and *understanding* of certain matters, situations, or truths in the Bible. Moses fasted and was given a revelation of the spirit of the Law. He got caught up on the mountain for 40 days in the glory of God and came down radiant! The spirit of the Law is compassion, grace, patience, abundant love, faithfulness, mercy, forgiveness, justice, holiness, righteousness. Fasting brings a revelation of God's covenant of Love and His perfect Law (see Exodus 34:28).

Elijah spent 40 days on a mountain also, as he fasted and waited on God—part of the time hiding in a cave. Sometimes we run in fear, get overwhelmed by people and circumstances and hide ourselves away. During these times, if we will pray and seek God's face in a fast, then He will reveal Himself to us in "mountain top" experiences. If you feel as though you are "living in a cave," start fasting for God's voice to speak to you as He did to Elijah! (see 1 Kings 19:8-9)

FASTING "BY APPOINTMENT"

In Antioch, the church leaders fasted and prayed before they "sent out" Paul and Barnabas. They wanted their choice to be God's choice, and also to ensure success of the Lord's work and mission. When Barnabas and Paul later established New Testament churches, they followed the same pattern in foreign cities where they ministered: the two fasted and prayed before commissioning and appointing elders in those cities (see Acts 13:3-4; 14:23).

Jesus prayed and (most probably) fasted before He appointed his apostles. He stayed up all night to pray.

One of those days Jesus went out to a mountainside to pray, and spent the night praying to God. When morning came, he called his disciples to him and chose twelve of them, whom he also designated apostles: (Luke 6:12-13).

HEAVENLY REWARDS

We don't fast for rewards, because that would be the wrong motivation. But in God's awesome abundance, He chooses to reward His children for sacrificial surrender through prayer and fasting. Jesus taught that we are not to be hypocritical, and do such acts only to impress men. Rather, we are to seek to bless God. That means much of our prayer and fasting is to be "hidden," and seen only by God. We are to pray and fast with an attitude of joy.

> *When you fast, do not look somber as the hypocrites do, for they disfigure their faces to show men they are fasting. I tell you the truth, they have received their reward in full. But when you fast, put oil on your head and wash your face, so that it will not be obvious to men that you are fasting, but only to your Father, who is unseen; and your Father, who sees what is done in secret will reward you* (Matthew 6:16-18).

Jesus further emphasizes through His teaching that prayer and fasting are like divine treasure, and this is expressed in Christ, who is the treasure of our hearts: *"For where your treasure is, there you heart will be also"* (Matthew 6:21).

THE ENEMY DOES IT TOO!

Make no mistake: satan understands the power of fasting, and he uses it for evil purposes! Ahab (King of Israel and husband of Jezebel) refused food whilst he lay in bed, as he had a tantrum and schemed his way toward killing Naboth so as to secure his vineyard.

> *So Ahab went home, sullen and angry because Naboth the Jezreelite had said, "I will not give you the inheritance of my fathers." He lay on his bed sulking and refused to eat (1 Kings 21:4).*

In Acts 23, we read of how the enemy blinded the Jewish people, and they vowed and committed together to a *total* fast until Paul was killed.

> *The next morning the Jews formed a conspiracy and bound themselves with an oath not to eat or drink until they had killed Paul. More than forty men were involved in this plot (Acts 23:12-13).*

We cannot finish this short study by exalting how the enemy uses one of God's most perfect, pure tools for overcoming! Prayer and fasting are so much on God's heart for His people. Join me in praying these words with all your heart:

Father, we come to You in total abandonment and surrender to Your perfect will. Lord, forgive us for the times we've been lazy and couldn't be bothered to fast and pray. Lord, forgive us for our pride and arrogance, for our selfish and vain ambitions, for ignoring the Great Commission and for making excuses for not fasting and praying.

Lord, help us to make a choice right now in support of You and against our flesh. Lord, we admit we are weak, but we stand on the truth of your Word: that Your strength is made perfect in our weakness. We want to fast, we want to be breakthrough believers, and we want to be like Jesus. We want to see the lost saved and the lame healed. We want to see our nations set ablaze with Your glory.

Oh, God, we are desperate for more of You. We are desperate to see You move in power in our lives and in the lives of all those around us. We are desperate and hungry for Your presence and for Your compassion; we just want to be like You, Jesus. There's nothing else for us, Lord, we just want more of You. You are the air we breathe.

Oh, God, purify us and bring Heaven to earth through these broken vessels. You are the reason that we live. We need You; desperately, earnestly we seek You. Come, Lord Jesus, and be our strength. Holy Spirit reveal the dross in us, burn it up and show us how to die to sin and selfishness, to give up our wills, our emotions and even our minds to you. Father, use us for Your glory and show us how to walk in grace. Teach us how to fast and pray. Rabbi, teach us, for Your sake and for the lost.

Amen.

APPENDIX II

Fasting Tips

[Some of this information was obtained or adapted from the book
"Fast forward" by Lou Engle]

*D*on't be too hard on yourself! If you start a fast and then give up midway, try not to view it as failure. Instead, focus on the time that you did manage to fast, and thank Jesus that you will be able to do it again in His grace!

COMMON SENSE FASTING

Be kind to your body for about a week before your fast. Cut down on caffeine, such as coffee, tea and Coca-Cola. Also, cut down on sugary snacks, and, gradually, reduce your food intake over this seven-day period.

TYPES OF FASTS

Complete Fast - Total abstinence from food and water.

Only do such a fast after a medical consultation. It's not recommended for more than three days: any longer time without water can shut down your kidneys! If you haven't done any fasting before, please don't start with a total fast—it's much wiser to try a Daniel fast first. Esther and Ezra called for full fasts; these were not only personal fasts, but also had a corporate element to them, as the whole nation fasted at the same time and produced miraculous results (see Ezra 8:21, 10:6; Esther 4:16).

"Daniel" Fast

Daniel fasted on fruit and vegetables. You can do a Daniel fast by cutting out "sweets and meats," and sticking to fruit, vegetables, juices and nuts. God will honor such a fast just as much as full-on fasting from food. Daniel fasted for three weeks to pray for his nation. A Daniel fast is a partial fast. In 1 Kings 17, Elijah did a partial fast; and John the Baptist also partially fasted through his diet of locusts and wild honey (see Matthew 3:4).

Juice Fast

You might feel unable to give up food and water completely. But most people can do a juice fast, which consists of drinking fruit and vegetable juices, like those of carrots, cranberrys and so forth.

Jesus Style - Extended Fast

A fast like the one Jesus did during His wilderness time will birth incredible, Jesus-style qualities in your life and ministry. Jesus abstained from all food (see Luke 4:1-2), but probably partook of liquids by drinking water. This is a "normal" fast. You might want to consider drinking distilled water, which will help flush impurities out of your system. Forty day fasts are very powerful. Please seek medical advice before you begin.

WHILE YOU ARE FASTING

* You may be tempted to eat—try not to give in.

* If you lead a very busy and demanding life, you may need to take the occasional Complan-type, liquid food to sustain you.

* Do take time to pray during your regular eating times! It can be frustrating if you fast, and then don't pray! As a mother of four, I find this quite challenging: to make meals and then not sit down with my family is difficult. Sometimes, I do sit with them, and then find my quiet time later in the evening. Don't be legalistic

about how and when you pray. Trust the Holy Spirit for His perfect timing. Remember, you can become the fast and not just be "fasting." Your lifestyle is the fast, so it's not always necessary to pray during a specific mealtime.

* Don't drink too many acidic juices, such as that of oranges. If you want to drink acidic juices, make sure to water them down well.

* Don't overload your system with too much sugar—even natural sugar. Apple juice is okay, but it's still quite sugary and may need to be diluted.

* Don't physically exhaust yourself. If you feel tired, then rest. My knees have sometimes buckled out from under me during a fast. At these times, it can be tempting to give in and stop fasting, so be sure to rest if necessary.

* Don't be cruel to yourself! If your body says, "I'm starving," then you need to tell it to "shut up." But, do not punish yourself if you do end up giving in.

* Do make specific prayer targets for your fast. However, don't take on responsibilities that aren't yours, but belong to God. Let God be God. You do your bit, and He will move in power. It's not your battle—it is His!

* Do set a timetable for the fast. It's wisest to start small. You may want to start by missing one meal, and then lead up to fasting once-a-week (either by missing lunch or dinner). The children of Israel observe a one-day fast on the Day of Atonement.

* Do give yourself time for Bible reading and to spend time with Jesus to enjoying His love. The spiritual opposition can be quite intense, so don't rely on your own strength; rest in your Father's loving arms when the going gets tough! Satan will try and attack you mentally, either through depression or a sense of heaviness and failure. Pray through to victory!

SIDE EFFECTS OF FASTING

After three days of fasting, you usually break through the initial "pain" barrier! Some unpleasant effects of fasting include headaches, nausea, dizziness, a stiff neck, and diarrhea.

BREAKING YOUR FAST

* Slow is safe

* Treat your body with kindness and respect

* Of course, you might want to indulge in a big juicy steak or a huge bar of chocolate. But you can safely break your fast with salad, yogurt, a small a piece of toast, or small helpings of fresh fruit.

* Remember that sometimes breakthrough comes after the fast, and not always during.

Endnotes

There is a Biblical example for a total abstinence from food and water for more than three days, but this took place in the literal glory of God! *"Moses was there with the LORD forty days and forty nights without eating bread or drinking water"* (Exodus 34:28).

Catherine Brown's Ministry

MILLION HOURS OF PRAISE

God has given me a vision to mobilize the church and the nations of the earth to worship Jesus for one million hours, and we at MILLION HOURS OF PRAISE believe that this worship will carry on past many millions of hours. Why are we doing this? Because Jesus is worth it!

GATEKEEPERS

GATEKEEPERS is a servant ministry entrusted to Catherine Brown with a vision to serve the Body of Christ and the lost through the active promotion and encouragement of prayer, worship, evangelism, and missions.

The vision for GATEKEEPERS has a strong emphasis on children and young people, but embraces the whole church across denominational lines and through all areas of social and cultural strata.

TO WRITE TO THE AUTHOR:

Gatekeepers, c/o 18 Castleview, West Kilbride, Ayrshire, KA23 9HD, Scotland, UK

TO BOOK CATHERINE FOR YOUR MEETING OR CONFERENCE PLEASE CONTACT:

tshofarblows@aol.com

www.millionhoursofpraise.com
www.gatekeepers.org.uk

Isbn:0-9740554-0-9

A light for your journey, a hope for your heart, a mission for your life.

Catherine Brown's openness and vulnerability in sharing her prophetic journey in *The Normal, The Deep and The Crazy* will warm your heart and bring great encouragement. Through her personal testimony, you will find that she paints a beautiful picture and profile of the character and gifting that is required to mould a prophetic vessel, fit for the Master's use. This book will enable many to rise up in courage to embrace the high calling of Christ that resides within them.

Order to:
www.gatekeepers.org.uk

Books to help you grow strong in Jesus

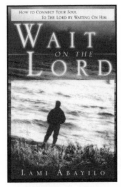

WAIT ON THE LORD

By Lami Abayilo

Have you been stuck in a world of containment? Are you tired of trying to find answers to life's questions? Do you want to discover the presence of God and enjoy an intimate relationship in Him? Then it is time to embark on the rich rewarding journey of waiting on the Lord. Go ahead! Unfold the pages of this wellspring of life and discover what transformation the presence of God can bring to your life. Plans will swap places. His presence will pour into you. You will know Him in a personal way. Your desires will be engulfed in the Word. All these and so much more will happen in your life because you dared to *Wait on the Lord.*

ISBN:88-89127-08-2

JOHNNY ROCKET AND HIS COMRADES IN THE FAITH

By Matthew Botsford

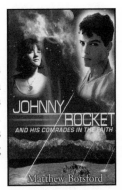

Join a young boy's imaginative adventures in his intergalactic spaceship, The Regatta, with his "comrades in the faith," as they discover new worlds and civilizations while seeking to "save the world" as only a boy can imagine. Danger, sabotage, miracles, healings, and manifestations follow Johnny Rocket in his journeys, all the while revealing exciting, Biblically based moral realities.

ISBN: 88-89127-07-4

Order Now from Destiny Image Europe
Telephone: +39 085 4716623- Fax +39 085 4716622
E-mail: ordini@eurodestinyimage.com

Internet: www.eurodestinyimage.com

Additional copies of this book and other book titles from DESTINY IMAGE EUROPE are available at your local bookstore.

For a complete list of our titles, visit us at

www.eurodestinyimage.com

Send a request for a catalog to:

Via Maiella, 1
66020 S. Giovanni Teatino (Ch) ITALY

* * * * * * * * ** * ** * ** * ** *

Are you an author?

Do you have a "today" God-given message?

CONTACT US

We will be happy to review your manuscript for a possible publishing.

publisher@eurodestinyimage.com